PRAISE FOR
SECRETS OF DYNAMIC COMMUNICATION

"I've spent over three decades immersed in the world of public speaking, and I still learned TONS of game-changing information from Ken's book. If you are a speaker or want to be one, you will give yourself an unfair advantage when you read *Secrets of Dynamic Communication*."

—ROBERT D. SMITH
Author of *20,000 Days and Counting*

"A must-read that reveals the Secrets Ken Davis has used to entertain and inspire audiences around the world."

—DUANE WARD
Founder/CEO, Premiere Speakers
Bureau

"As I meet powerful communicators in various walks of life, one theme is constant—they identify the training of Ken Davis as the ignition point of their professional career. If you are a Sunday school teacher, salesman, business owner, coach, politician, pastor, artist, corporate trainer, social entrepreneur, or anyone who desires having a voice that is heard, this book can transform your impact. You will find *Secrets of Dynamic Communication* to be an indispensable source for preparing and delivering your message in a way that can change lives—including yours."

—DAN MILLER
Author of *New York Times* best-
selling *48 Days to the Work You Love*

"Because of my storytelling role with Chick-fil-A, I am often invited to speak with various groups about a wide range of topics. Throughout the years, I have found Ken Davis' SCORRE method of communication to be an invaluable resource. As communicators, we owe it to those who follow to learn from the wisdom that Ken shares in this book. You will be both encouraged and inspired as you begin to better understand the *Secrets of Dynamic Communication*."

—DAN T. CATHY
President and COO, Chick-fil-A, Inc.

"Ken Davis is the acknowledged gold standard of professional speakers and now, he is generously sharing his tricks of the trade. *Secrets of Dynamic Communication* is an instant classic and will be the 'go-to' book on effective presentation for decades to come."

—ANDY ANDREWS
New York Times Best-Selling Author
of *The Traveler's Gift* and *The Noticer*

"It's been my joy and privilege to travel extensively with Ken and watch as he holds an audience in the palm of his hand through his exquisite gift of storytelling. He is a master communicator and his method for preparation has impacted thousands of speakers, including me."

—SHEILA WALSH
Author of *God Loves Broken People*

"For most of my life, I couldn't imagine anything more terrifying than public speaking. But then I discovered SCORRE and Ken Davis. SCORRE gave me the tools I needed to craft a focused and powerful presentation. And Ken Davis? He gave me the heart and confidence to deliver it with passion."

—MICHELE CUSHATT
Speaker, Author,
& Communications Coach

"Ken Davis is a master communicator who has inspired thousands, myself included. Learning his SCORRE method has transformed the way I prepare and deliver speeches. Highly recommended!"

—CRYSTAL PAINE
Author of *Say Goodbye to Survival Mode*,
MoneySavingMom.com

"Sitting through Ken's SCORRE Conference with the entire Women of Faith team was an absolute delight, but I had no idea what a sharp tool his methods would become in my tool belt. A month later I sat down to develop the outline for my next book, and what normally would have taken weeks I managed to accomplish in two hours! As they say in the recovery movement, *this WORKS if you work it!* I've recommended this book to all of the aspiring writers and speakers that I personally coach, and I'm thrilled that we now have this updated version. I consider it the 'effective communicator's bible.'"

—SHANNON ETHRIDGE, M.A.
Author of twenty books including
the Every Woman's Battle series and
The Fantasy Fallacy

"If you use your voice to earn a living and want to make yourself heard above the seamless chatter of the industry, *Secrets of Dynamic Communication* is decisively for you. With over twenty years of experience, I've seen countless people benefit from learning and implementing these secrets. Bottom line: if you are looking for a competitive edge this is a must-read."

—TIM GRABLE
CEO & Owner, The Grable Group

"After learning the SCORRE method, it's now blatantly obvious what separates a good communicator from a GREAT communicator who can inspire, persuade, and move people into action."

—STU MCLAREN
Co-Founder, WishList Member

"Before, I was just a guy with a powerful story who covered up my lack of speaking skills by compensating with passion. After mastering the SCORRE method, I have been transformed into a confident, professional, public speaker who is now equipped to perform high paying keynote presentations."

—CLIFF RAVENSCRAFT
Podcaster, Blogger & Speaker,
PodcastAnswerMan.com

"Ken Davis is a role model for effective communication: he doesn't just understand it, he practices it at the highest levels, impacting not only his listeners and readers but other professional speakers like myself who continually learn and marvel at his skill and impact. Read this book: you couldn't ask for a better teacher."

—MARK SANBORN
President, Sanborn & Associates, Inc.,
An Idea studio for leadership
development

"How can a fantastic book get even better? When Ken Davis applies his well-honed approach to communication to an already-best seller, words pop—ideas emerge—focus wins! Most people are terrified of speaking in public, whether to a small group, in a business setting or at church. No more! Pick up this book, follow Ken through the pages and come out on the other side with clarity and confidence that you can speak with purpose in the various arenas of your life."

—ELISA MORGAN
Speaker, Author of *The Beauty of Broken*, & Publisher, www.fullfill.org

"We utilized Ken's team with the teaching of the SCORRE method for our speaker team for Women of Faith. Going through this process changed the way the individuals prepared their messages to be shared at large arena events. This method has also helped me think about how I communicate to staff or in formal presentations."

—CAROL NYGREN
Managing Director, Women of Faith

"Ken is not only an amazing communicator but also a brilliant teacher. He takes the complicated process of crafting a speech and breaks it down into a manageable process. This book gives step- by-step instruction that will enhance both the power and the connectivity of your very next speech."

—LYSA TERKEURST
New York Times Best-Selling Author,
National Speaker, and President of
Proverbs 31 Ministries

SECRETS OF DYNAMIC COMMUNICATION

PREPARE *with* FOCUS,
DELIVER *with* CLARITY,
SPEAK *with* POWER

KEN DAVIS

W PUBLISHING GROUP

AN IMPRINT OF THOMAS NELSON

Published in Nashville, Tennessee, by W Publishing Group. W Publishing is a registered trademark of Thomas Nelson, Inc.

All Scripture quotations, unless otherwise noted, are taken from the Holy Bible, New International Version®, NIV®. Copyright © 1973, 1978, 1984, by Biblica, Inc.™. Used by permission of Zondervan. All rights reserved worldwide. www.zondervan.com

Library of Congress Cataloging-in-Publication Data Available Upon Request

ISBN 978-0-8499-2190-2

Printed in the United States of America
13 14 15 16 17 RRD 6 5 4 3 2 1

Contents

Foreword

Public speaking.

These words scare most people. Rightfully so. At one time, they scared me too. But unless you live in absolute solitude or silence, communication is an unavoidable part of life. And how well you do it matters more than you think. Few skills directly impact your success as a leader, writer, coworker, spouse, or parent like that of communication. Bomb, and you're likely to hear about it. Deliver, and your audience will never forget.

I spent the summer before my sophomore year in college as part of a group service project in Galveston, Texas. Each week my team visited a different church in the area and led Vacation Bible School. It was fun, rewarding work. In addition, I was assigned to a local church where I lived with the pastor, his wife, and their two children. The adults were both in their fifties and made me feel right at home.

After I had been there for about a month, the pastor approached me one day and casually said, "Mike, Rhonda and I are going out of town next weekend. I'd like for you to lead the service on Sunday and preach for me."

Panic. I immediately felt the color drain from my face. I was terrified. "But, I've never spoken in public," I stammered.

"Don't worry. You'll do fine," he chuckled. "There's a first time for everything." Then he got up and walked out of the room. Evidently, refusing the assignment was not an option!

I remember studying like crazy during that week. I read the Bible and poured over commentaries. I outlined the points I wanted to make, then revised the outline with great deliberation. Dissatisfied, I threw it away and started over. This process repeated itself several times over the course of those days. In the meantime, I felt sick and couldn't sleep. What had been rewarding work became a fearful, painful exercise. I practiced in front of a mirror, but didn't really know what I was doing and had no idea where to turn for help. I dreaded facing the congregation on Sunday.

When the moment of truth came, I delivered my presentation. Just as my friend predicted, I did fine. My sermon wasn't great, but I got through it. I survived, as did my audience. But that day I learned a valuable lesson. Communication—public speaking, in particular—doesn't just happen. It's a hard-earned skill requiring study and diligent practice. I needed to either take it seriously or find something else to do.

Little did I know it at the time, but the years that followed would provide me many opportunities for practice. I wrote a couple of books (one a best seller), worked as a literary agent, launched my own publishing company, started working at Thomas Nelson Publishers, Inc., eventually became CEO of that same company, and raised five daughters alongside my wife, Gail. Opportunities for public speaking and communication abounded! I made hundreds of presentations and conducted thousands of radio, television, and phone interviews. By nature of volume, I no longer felt terrified at the prospect of public speaking. But the amount of work I put into each presentation was significant. I couldn't keep up. And although I improved, I wanted to get even better—I needed to.

Enter Ken Davis. One of the country's most sought-after motivational speakers. Ken and his wife, Diane, lived in the same town as Gail and I, and we became quick friends. I heard him talk about the SCORRE Conference, a conference he had founded and been faithfully leading for more than twenty-five years. I heard his passion and knew he had a gift for crafting and delivering messages that literally changed lives. I'd seen him do it! My curiosity piqued; Ken invited Gail and me to attend his conference in 2010. I couldn't refuse.

We were blown away. If only I'd learned this sooner! I could have shortened the learning curve by years and accelerated my proficiency significantly. I'm not exaggerating when I say I've learned and improved more in the past two years under Ken's guidance than I did in the thirty years of presentations before. Even though I regret not doing it sooner, I'm glad I didn't wait to take the next step.

My time at the SCORRE Conference reenergized my love for writing and speaking. I immediately put into practice the SCORRE process, and discovered my messages had the clarity and power I'd always wanted. Not only that, it gave me the courage I needed to take a huge step of faith. On April 11, 2011, I stepped down as CEO of Thomas Nelson. I now make my living as a communicator, something the terrified college sophomore never thought he'd do!

Whether you are a professional speaker, pastor, corporate executive, author—or are just passionate about a message—you can take your communication skills to the next level. Ken's SCORRE system truly revolutionized my public presentations. The good news? What I learned from him sits right here, in this book. Within these pages, you'll learn how to:

- dramatically reduce your prep time,
- communicate with more clarity and focus,
- increase your ability to connect with the audience, and
- craft speeches that leave an impact.

I still have room to grow and want to get better. But Ken Davis and his SCORRE method launched me further than I could've hoped. It's influenced just about everything I do: leading, writing, speaking, blogging . . . you name it. My life and message are more clear, focused, and powerful as a result of what you now hold in your hand.

Pull up a chair, open your mind to learn, and prepare to be stretched and empowered. You will be the better for it, as will your audience. And who knows? You just might be someone's guest speaker this weekend. This book will show you how to do it.

—MICHAEL HYATT
New York Times Best-Selling Author
Former CEO, Thomas Nelson Publishers

Acknowledgments

I wish to give special thanks to the people who have made the publication of this book possible. My grateful thanks to a team of associates whose quest for excellence has helped refine the SCORRE process over the years, in particular our SCORRE Conference coaches. For nearly thirty years, I have benefited from the insight and collaboration of these excellent communicators. No doubt, I am a better presenter for it. To Brian Scheer and Joy Groblebe, who relentlessly pushed me to write this book. What you hold in your hands would not have happened without their perseverance. A special thanks to writer and friend Michele Cushatt for her editing and collaboration. Thanks to Matt Baugher for his belief in this material and encouragement as a friend and publisher. To Haddon Robinson and Lloyd Perry for the inspiration of their excellent books and teaching. A special thanks to the thousands of SCORRE Conference participants who have put into practice the secrets revealed in this book and as a result made a powerful impact in their world. Thank you to my friend and business partner, Michael Hyatt. Your passion for excellence in communication has inspired me. Thank you for your help in shaping this material for a broader audience.

Introduction

When I first submitted this book for publication, the editor asked a critical question: Who would want to read a book on the secrets of dynamic communication? The first and most obvious answer is, anyone who has something to say and wants to say it well. But that only includes those who live on planet Earth, and I didn't want to leave anyone out.

Speakers, nonfiction authors, salespersons, entertainers, preachers, moms, dads, husbands, wives, corporate leaders, and political figures will find that the secrets of dynamic communication can revolutionize their ability to develop powerful presentations that persuade and move people to action.

So who else would benefit from the secrets of dynamic communication? The very first "secret" will become an essential tool for anyone who makes plans, sets goals, and wants to live with powerful focus rather than stumble aimlessly without purpose or direction. So if you are headed somewhere, want to achieve something, and desire to live to your fullest potential, the principles in this book that lead to good communication also lead to good life. And that probably covers those who might live on other planets.

You won't find abstract theories here—only step-by-step instructions that will enable you to prepare with focus, deliver with clarity, and speak with power: skills associated with only the very best speakers.

The book will enable you to focus your objectives and organize your material so that you can deliver your message with unshakable confidence.

As you read you will discover that the secrets of dynamic communication need not be secrets at all. These principles have been tested and proven true by hundreds of speakers all over the world, and they will work for you too.

The secret is out.

PART I

THE PREPARATION: THE SCORRE PROCESS

The Most Important Ingredient

Focus, Focus, Focus

What is your secret?"

Every time I turned around, someone asked me that question. At the back of the room after an event, in letters from fans, during media interviews, and even today after more than forty years of professional speaking, I'm asked, "What is your secret?" That's why I wrote this book.

But before we get to the secrets, a little history.

I think I was born with the communication gene. Most people fear public speaking. I have loved doing it as far back as I can remember. When a radio interviewer asked when I first started making people laugh and listen, I answered, "When the doctor slapped me on the rear and said it's a boy."

During my junior year in high school, Francis W. Peterson, my English teacher, inspired/blackmailed me to enter a speech contest. She also encouraged my participation in class plays and debate. Once I had tasted the rush of rhetoric and the joy of creating laughter, there was no turning back.

After graduating from high school I studied to be a pastor, one of the most challenging communication occupations there is. Congregations across the country still celebrate the day I chose not to follow that path. Instead, I found myself fielding calls from people in all walks of life who had heard me speak and wanted me to come and make presentations. I developed a high school assembly program called "Nothing but the Best" that I delivered to nearly a million students across the country. I was invited to speak at some of the top corporations in the country, as well as in many churches.

As my career took off, people who were interested in honing their speaking skills began to ask: "What is your secret? How is it possible for you to speak to such a variety of audiences and hold their attention? Can you teach me how to do it?" I was embarrassed to confess that I didn't know the secret. I didn't even know there was a secret. I thought it just came naturally. Eventually the question could no longer be ignored. I did some research and began observing the best communicators in the country to discover what common denominator kept them in constant demand. What separated them from the average after-dinner drone? What gave one speaker the ability to empower and persuade so effectively when another could only inspire yawns?

At first the evidence led me to believe that the secret was in the "dynamics" of communication, that spark of enthusiasm, wit, humor, and animation that was the mark of so many great communicators. So we put together our first conference, called it "Dynamic Communicators Workshop," and taught our students how to develop those dynamics. It was at that workshop we discovered the real secret. Although the "dynamics" were common denominators to all of the most gifted communicators, there was something else, something less visible that set the best apart from everyone else.

If I were to ask you what that ingredient was, what would your answer be? Humor? Voice inflection? Interesting material? Good illustrations? Dynamic personality? Grab your highlighter. All of those are important, but the real secret to effective, dynamic speaking is . . .

FOCUS

When we conducted our first workshop, now called the SCORRE Conference, 90 percent of the curriculum consisted of lectures and breakout sessions that taught those physical, dynamic aspects of presentation. Yet at the end of the workshop every student who attended identified the most valuable takeaway of the week was a forty-minute session on how to prepare a presentation with a single focused objective: focus. Everything else seemed to hang on this one teachable skill.

....

It is in seclusion that the great communicators carefully craft that great public performance.

....

It's now been over thirty years since that first SCORRE Conference. Thousands of students have confirmed that if you want people to listen, learn, and take action, you must speak with crystal-clear focus. So why is it such a secret? Because focus doesn't happen in public on a well-lit platform. It happens in secret. In the quiet of your home or office.

FOCUS

We watch an amazing quarterback throw a perfect pass for the winning touchdown and wonder, "What is the secret to such precision?" And the answer is so unglamorous. It is hours of unseen practice, developing the "mundane" foundational basics such as how to hold the ball, how to stand, and how to develop the most efficient throwing motion. I wipe tears from my eyes as I listen to an orchestra bring a concert hall of patrons to their feet in wild applause. What is their secret? Years of playing scales, practicing the nuance of timing and volume. It's a secret because we don't see it. We just benefit from the result. It is in seclusion that the great communicators carefully craft that great public performance. In private they practice the secrets of dynamic communication that effectively drive their message home.

It is only after that focused preparation they can step on the platform to speak with confidence, move people to action, and change lives. And those of us who aspire to be great wonder, what is their secret? A relentless commitment to . . .

FOCUS

Unfortunately the most widely excepted philosophy of communication is something quite different.

Shortly before I graduated from high school, I was invited to go deer hunting with the men from our community. Most of our neighbors and friends owned small farms and had little income. They depended on this hunt to help feed their families during the long Minnesota winters. To be invited to this ritual was an honor I had dreamed of for years. I can still feel the excitement of that frosty November opening day of deer season. A dozen men were lined up on a road prepared to march through a stand of timber and scare the ticks off any deer that might be hiding there. At the other end of the forest another group of men were posted in tree stands prepared to shoot any deer that tried to escape.

What a thrill. This was my rite of passage. I was now a trusted member of the adult providers in our community. I had hiked less than a hundred yards into the woods when a shot rang out. The bullet from that shot hit a tree only inches from my face and the splattering bark left welts on my cheek. Dazed, I remember thinking, *That was close.*

I took a few more steps and a second shot zipped above my head. As bits of leaf and branch landed on my shoulders, my naive young mind concluded, *What a coincidence. Two close calls.* The third shot followed almost immediately and came so close to my ear that I felt heat as it passed. I needed no more evidence. My mind screamed, *Someone is shooting at you!* My body responded.

I dived for the ground as bullet after bullet buzzed above my head. When the shooting stopped I looked up and could see the man who had been firing. He had used up all his ammunition and was in the process of reloading his gun. With a vocabulary I am not proud of, and screams of outrage that could be heard throughout the county, I managed to convince him that it would be hazardous to his health to shoot in my direction again.

Here's my point. This dangerous person should never have been allowed out of his pickup truck. I'm sure he was filled with enthusiasm and was probably using excellent equipment, but he lacked focus. Evidently his philosophy of hunting was, "There are deer in the woods somewhere. If I just shoot enough bullets in there, I'm bound to hit something!" Yeah, like me!

....

If you aim at nothing, you will hit nothing every time.

....

This is a dangerous and ineffective hunting strategy. It is also an ineffective communication strategy. Yet I am convinced that it is the unconscious, unspoken approach of many sincere communicators. "There are people out there everywhere," they reason. "If I just shoot enough information in their direction, something is bound to hit."

Nothing could be further from the truth. If you aim at nothing, you will hit nothing every time.

How can you expect an audience to get what you are aiming at if you don't even know yourself? In the first few moments of your speech, the audience decides whether you are worth listening to. If they sense a lack of direction or focus, you might as well pack your bags and go home because that's what their minds will do. Too often we end up preparing ineffectual shotgun messages, desperately wanting something—anything—to get through to the audience. We try to say it all, and end up communicating nothing.

....

70 percent of the people leaving a presentation had
no idea what had been communicated.

....

Several years ago we did an informal survey of over two thousand people who had just listened to speakers in various communication settings. Although each survey was conducted less than fifteen minutes after the presentation, over 70 percent of the people leaving a presentation had no idea what had been communicated. Some could remember a joke or illustration, but most couldn't identify any purpose or direction for the talk. Why had the speaker even bothered to talk?

That isn't the sad statistic. We also interviewed the speakers and discovered that more than 50 percent of the speakers could not articulate an objective or FOCUS to their talk. They didn't know what they were trying to say or accomplish. No wonder the audience didn't know either!

That's why a dynamic presentation is secondary to a focused presentation. What good is it to be dynamic about nothing? What good are illustrations that go nowhere or interesting material that ends up on a dead-end street? Dynamics and theatrics without focus are merely entertainment. Nothing wrong with that, unless you are trying to communicate. Novels and plays have a plot, trips have a destination, life has a purpose. If you want to communicate, the single most important ingredient is an unmistakable aiming point and a careful plan to hit it. FOCUS, FOCUS, FOCUS. Focused purpose. Focused preparation. Focused presentation.

....

Dynamics and theatrics without focus are merely entertainment.

....

THE CONSEQUENCES OF UNFOCUSED COMMUNICATION

A new generation of speakers and leaders sometimes question the effectiveness of establishing a crystal-clear objective and constructing a speech that will lead to that objective. They believe that a smorgasbord of thoughts regurgitated in a creative manner will more effectively instruct, persuade, or encourage an audience. My question is, are you trying to communicate something? If so, then why not know what that something is and move people toward it? When pressed on what it is they want to communicate, many don't know. At best their response indicates that there are many "things" they want to say.

The same philosophy behind effective communication is utilized to function successfully in our day-to-day lives. When driving, we choose a destination and then choose the roads that will lead us there. When hungry, we take action to sate that hunger. In every case, all efforts are focused on one specific target or goal. If you find yourself in a strange airport and need power for your iPhone, your focused objective is to find an outlet. Only when you achieve that objective and finally slide the charging cord into an outlet and hear that wonderful "ding," can you relax and then choose a new objective.

This objective force drives our lives. In communication it is so powerful that if we don't set a focus for our presentation, an unconscious one will take over. Here are some of the vague, power-stealing, unconscious objectives that can rear their heads and steal power from a speech:

- I hope they like me.
- I need to fill the time.
- I need to get through the material.
- I want to impress the audience.
- I want to regurgitate my research.
- I want to make my quota.
- I must cover every item on the agenda.

The insidious nature of these diversions is that they negatively affect every aspect of a presentation and its outcome without you even being aware of it. If your unconscious objective is to be liked, you will unconsciously design and deliver a speech to meet that objective. People will like you! But is that what you wanted to accomplish with your presentation? If so, Hollywood might be a better career choice.

The power of unconscious objectives was graphically illustrated on another of my hunting trips. Years ago I exchanged my guns for a bow and arrow. I wanted to make hunting more of a challenge. I practiced until I was able to put all my arrows in an apple at twenty yards, and on several occasions I even split arrows in the target because I was shooting them so close together. The only way to achieve that kind of accuracy is to concentrate, not on the apple, but on one tiny spot right in the center of the apple. I worked at this concentration until it became second nature.

One day while hunting, I peeked over a ridge to discover one of the biggest bucks I had ever seen standing only yards away completely unaware of my presence. This deer was every hunter's dream. His horns looked like trees. To be successful I had to shoot an arrow in an area about the size of a small paper plate just behind his front shoulder. There was no way I could miss. At this range I could hit a fifty-cent piece every time. I could picture those monstrous horns adorning my den as I pulled back the bow and released the arrow. It flew as if in slow motion and struck the deer . . . in the horns! Instead of picking a tiny spot to aim at, I hit the object of my focus.

Nothing will create more fear and anxiety than agonizing over whether the audience will like you or not.

Without conscious thought, I had concentrated on the horns, and that is exactly where my arrow stuck. That deer is probably still wearing the arrow ornament today, telling his grandchildren the story about the crazy guy with a sharp stick and a lack of focus.

In the early days of my career, my unconscious objective was "I hope they like me." I was working with youth and trying to communicate a very important message of faith. Because I was unfocused in my preparation, I was hitting the horns instead of the heart. My unconscious objective was met. They did like me, but I wasn't getting my message across. One night, I overheard a parent who was picking up her child ask, "What did Ken talk about tonight?" to which the student responded, "I don't know, but he was sure good." I no longer take this as a compliment. Good at what? Good at entertaining maybe, but certainly not communication.

Nothing will create more fear and anxiety than agonizing over whether the audience will like you or not. There are many great organizations out there designed to help people get over the fear of speaking. According to surveys this fear is second only to death, followed closely in our home by the fear of spiders. Understanding two facts can help minimize the obsession with being liked and the fear of speaking that is married to it. First, confidence comes from focused preparation. Second, communication is not about you.

Communication is not about you or what people will think about you or how well you will perform. Communication is about the people sitting in front of you. It's about giving to them, helping them, instructing them, and persuading them of something that will enrich their lives.

Dave was one of our SCORRE students who was on the ground floor of developing a medical delivery program that would benefit both physicians and patients. In essence it was the forerunner to HMOs. Part of his job was making presentations to doctors and patient advocate groups to convince them of the value of the system. There was one problem: Dave hated public speaking. After I had worked with Dave for several days, he told me, "I feel like I am so vulnerable in front of every group I speak to. What if I blow it? What will they think of me?"

Communication is not about you or what people will think about you or how well you will perform. Communication is about the people sitting in front of you. It's about giving to them, helping them, instructing them, and persuading them of something that will enrich their lives.

Here was a man who was offering a new product that would save millions of dollars for both the consumer and the provider, and yet his major concern was, "What will they think of me?" I remember leaning across the table and telling Dave, "It is not about you! You are not there to get personal approval; you are there to offer amazing benefits to your listeners. Instead of thinking about what they think about you, think about what you are giving to them."

After that Dave never looked back. The power of his presentations was multiplied, his sales soared, and he actually began to enjoy speaking.

THE SECRET FOR ACHIEVING FOCUS

I have watched thousands of men and women who have attended our SCORRE Conference discover the power of focused communication.

This process that is such a natural part of our everyday lives is also essential to good communication. The sculptor who conceives of a beautiful image she wishes to share with the public begins with a solid hunk of granite. All of the granite is good granite, yet to bring the image to life she must start chipping away perfectly good granite. Only by getting rid of what doesn't contribute to the image is she able to bring that image to life. The same is true when preparing a talk. To make it as clear and powerful as possible, it is necessary to know exactly what you want to accomplish and then keep only material that will contribute to the objective.

Hadden Robinson, a gifted communicator who has taught thousands of young ministers the principles of communication, says that "a sermon should be more like a bullet than a buckshot."[1] This "bullet" principle applies to all kinds of speaking.

SPEAKING WITH AN OBJECTIVE IS ESSENTIAL TO GOOD COMMUNICATION.

All good books on communication agree with Robinson's point. The question is, how does a speaker craft this objective bullet? One of the reasons why this focus concept has remained a secret is because it is not readily observable from the platform; instead, it is carefully crafted in private, during the preparation process. On the platform you see the results, the touchdown pass, the standing ovation. Another reason it often remains a secret is that determining the focus for a talk is hard work. To some, like Robinson, it seems to come naturally, a part of their giftedness. But the rest of us need some help.

Traditionally the methodology for preparing a speech looked like this. One would first study and research the subject to be covered. During this process the speaker would list all the things he wanted to say. He would then organize that material in the order it was to be delivered and he was ready to speak.

Too often, little consideration was given to the secret of dynamic communication: focus! The SCORRE methodology is different and vitally important. Our process also requires study and research of the subject. It also gives value to creative brainstorming as you list all the things you want to say in your talk. But once that is done SCORRE insists that the speaker must ask the most important question of all.

"Why!

Why do I want to say all these things? What do I want to accomplish?" The answer to those questions identifies the singular purpose. However, finding the answers to those questions can be difficult. And, in some cases, it changes the construction of the speech. Once you are sure of that focus, you will want to eliminate anything that doesn't contribute to it.

In this book you will learn a method for preparing messages that, like a scope, forces the speaker to prepare with an absolute, pinpointed focus. The preparation method is called SCORRE. The two primary functions of the SCORRE process are as follows:

1. It serves as a scope to force the speaker to focus on a single objective.
2. It serves as a logical grid forcing the speaker to make sense and lead the audience to the objective.

Don't be afraid of the word *force* used in the description of these functions. Like changing your grip on a golf club forces a new, more effective swing and lower scores, this uncomfortable process will change your preparation method and raise the scores of your presentations. This method works whether you are preparing a thirty-minute talk or a five-minute speech. It works whether you have a week to prepare or ten minutes to prepare.

Over the last three decades we have trained some of the best communicators in the country to use SCORRE. From start-up entrepreneurs to the top executives of Fortune 500 companies, from leaders of international organizations to ministry personnel who have to make presentations several times a week, from professional athletes to motivational speakers from as far away as New Zealand and South Africa. Students from all backgrounds and levels of experience have found the SCORRE method to be central to renewed excellence in their speaking, and for many SCORRE has been instrumental in helping launch their careers. Below is a brief overview of how the SCORRE process works.

But wait!

Just in case you're feeling some resistance, stick with me for a few more moments. Understand that SCORRE is a "basic" function carefully designed to help you build a foundation of focus and logic on which to construct a speech. Don't resist the process because it seems simplistic and restrictive. It is! But only to guide you to focus as you prepare. Once you achieve that focus, you are free to be as creative as you wish in your delivery of the message. Nothing in the book is designed to change your style or restrict your creativity, but rather to bring the power of focus to your creativity. If you will commit to the process, I guarantee you will be free to communicate with more clarity and power than you have ever known.

....

Nothing in the book is designed to change your style or restrict your creativity, but rather to bring the power of focus to your creativity.

....

So here we go.

SCORRE is an acronym that describes the basic process for developing any talk. It is also the process I used to write twelve books and plan the details of a successful career. (More about that later.) Here's the breakdown of what the acronym stands for:

S = Subject
C = Central Theme
O = Objective
R = Rationale
R = Resources
E = Evaluation

Choosing a **Subject** and narrowing that subject to a **Central Theme** helps the speaker determine what he wants to talk about. It also serves to narrow the focus of the talk to a manageable amount of information. You can see from the illustration of the hourglass that this part of the process narrows down the broader possibilities and aims the speech in a specific direction.

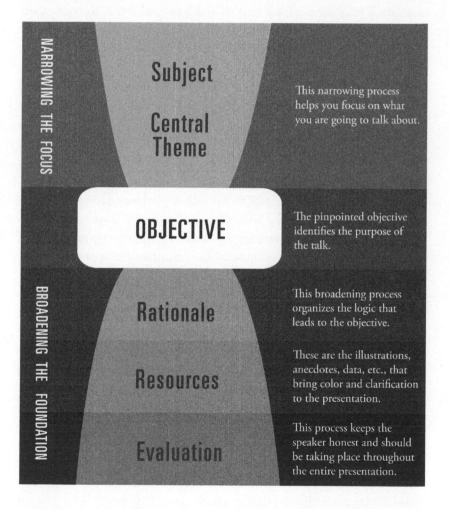

NARROWING THE FOCUS

Subject

Central Theme

This narrowing process helps you focus on what you are going to talk about.

OBJECTIVE

The pinpointed objective identifies the purpose of the talk.

BROADENING THE FOUNDATION

Rationale

This broadening process organizes the logic that leads to the objective.

Resources

These are the illustrations, anecdotes, data, etc., that bring color and clarification to the presentation.

Evaluation

This process keeps the speaker honest and should be taking place throughout the entire presentation.

Writing the **Objective** in a simple sentence forces the speaker to consider the single purpose of the talk. When the speaker clearly understands the objective of the talk, the likelihood of effective communication increases exponentially. In the following pages you will learn how to write an objective sentence that articulates the pinpoint focus of your speech. There should be only one objective for each talk.

Building powerful **Rationale** provides the logical framework for persuasion, instruction, or encouragement. The rationale is the logical content of your presentation that should lead the listener to your objective. Just as choosing the subject and central theme helped you narrow your focus to a single objective, the rationale is the structure of your talk that leads the audience to that objective.

Resources bring life to the presentation by adding light, color, and clarity. They keep the listener interested. Resources personalize what might otherwise seem like abstract ideas. Resources put flesh and blood on the dry bones of data and facts. Resources may be research results, illustrations, personal stories, humor . . . anything that clarifies your rationale and holds the attention of your audience.

If I simply tell you that SCORRE is basic and foundational, it's very possible you might miss my point. But the "resource" illustration I used of the pro quarterback practicing his passes highlights the value of that foundation. It provides an example of how the principle works in another arena. Resources help the listener "feel" what you are describing.

Evaluation is a process of self-examination. It causes the speaker to ask repeatedly, "Do I know what I am talking about?" and keeps him or her focused on the objective. Later we will talk about the value of using evaluation from the moment of a speech's conception until you contemplate the success of your finished presentation over a steaming cup of coffee.

Once you have the SCORRE process committed to memory and firmly in your grasp, you will discover that each of these steps can actually function more like portals. For some speeches you will be so sure of your focus that you start by determining your objective sentence first. In a corporate setting a manager might be required to present a list of points provided by a superior. In that situation you would begin with that list of rationale and then ask yourself, "Why am I giving this? How will it empower, motivate, or encourage my team?" The answer to those questions will determine your objective.

But for now let's follow the process in the order presented here.

REVIEW

You should commit a few key facts to memory before you move on to the next chapter. The following review is designed to help you get these basics firmly in your mind. You will be using them throughout this book.

1. What are the two primary functions of the SCORRE process?

   a. It serves as a scope to force the speaker to focus on a single

   _____.

   b. It serves as a _____ framework forcing the speaker to make sense.

2. The development of the subject and central theme _____ the talk to a manageable amount of information.

3. The subject and central theme will represent what the speaker wants to _____.

4. The objective pinpoints the _____ of the talk.

5. The rationale are more commonly known as the _____ of the talk, and should lead the listener to the objective.

6. The resources _____ the rationale, bring _____ to the talk, and make it interesting.

7. The evaluation gives the speaker an opportunity to assess the talk's effectiveness in reaching the _____.

Answers: 1a. objective 1b. logical 2. narrow 3. talk about 4. purpose 5. points 6. clarify, color 7. objective

Establishing the Subject and Central Theme

What Are You Talking About?

"Everything I say reminds me of something else."[1]
—LOWELL THOMAS

I believe in the power of focus. Any concerted effort to keep a speech confined to a single objective will dramatically improve that presentation. The lack of such effort can destroy the potential power of your talk.

I saw this illustrated in a unique way in Alaska. While there I visited a remote camp powered by electricity generated from a stream so small you could jump across it. At one point the owner forced the stream through a narrow opening just several feet across. There he placed a paddle wheel. The paddle wheel powered a generator, which in turn provided the electricity for the entire camp. Two years later I returned to find the camp had been destroyed. The stream had flooded and raged unrestricted over its banks.

When the water was channeled and focused it had provided power for the entire complex, but the uncontrolled/unfocused rambling of the same stream brought destruction.

I once spent a delightful evening listening to the late Lowell Thomas speak at a benefit dinner. It soon became obvious that it would be an evening of entertainment rather than instruction or motivation. In the midst of telling fascinating stories of his travels, this amazing man paused. "Forgive me," he chuckled, "but everything I say reminds me of something else."

Well said. At best, the temptation to ramble is difficult to resist. Without proper preparation, it is impossible. I'm sure Mr. Thomas's "objective" that evening was to entertain us. He brilliantly achieved that objective. Rarely is entertainment the objective of the average communicator. Most often our intent is to instruct, encourage, motivate, or call an audience to action. Following a rabbit trail of thoughts is not conducive to any of these objectives.

The words on this page are not what I wrote originally. What you are reading on this page was likely, at one time, two pages. It was only after rewriting five or six times and having the editor trim the final bits of fat from the text that it was focused enough for your reading.

I wanted to include a hilarious illustration of the angel and the worm, not because it would contribute to the objective of this book but because it was so clever and you might think me clever as well.

You, too, will want to present all the results of your study or research simply because it took so long, you learned so much. It seems a waste not to share everything you learned. Don't do it. Trim the fat! Know what the "heart of the matter" is and get to it. Your time and the listeners' time is precious.

So how does one stay focused and prepare a talk that will hit the mark? That is what the core of this book is all about. Powerful and persuasive speakers know the secret. They may not use the exact methods described in this book, but to the last one they are focused and organized. They know where they are going and how to bring the audience with them. That is what SCORRE will help you do.

I would like to suggest that the best way to read this material is to prepare a simple speech as you go. Don't try to do a thesis on the social consequences of ladybug infestations on Western culture. Later chapters will detail how the SCORRE system works to prepare everything from an annual report to writing a book, but keep it simple at first.

You will immediately experience the frustration of "forcing" yourself to a single focus, but if you stick with it, you will also begin to see the power that comes with such a discipline.

S = SUBJECT

The first step in preparing a focused speech is to choose a single subject from the endless possibilities available—marriage, parenting, camping, anything. This may sound overly simplistic, yet every year I hear hundreds of presentations that are actually several presentations on several subjects all wrapped into one confusing and often mind-numbing talk.

Your subject should be expressed in one or two words. Make the words broad enough to include what you want to talk about yet narrow enough to avoid a complete description of your entire talk.

Starting with a broad subject makes it easier to organize your thoughts as you focus your speech. It also makes it easier to determine the objective of your talk when you are not sure at first what that objective might be. Here are some examples of possible subjects:

- Marketing
- Love
- Fear
- Branding
- Social media
- Rabies
- Faith
- Rashes
- Relationships
- Office decorum
- Scuba diving

Before you choose your subject consider these guidelines:

1. THE SUBJECT MUST TOUCH YOUR AUDIENCE.

You would not do a message on parenting to a room full of college singles. You would not give a presentation on the strategies of big game hunting to a room full of animal rights activists. On the other hand, if there is an elephant in the room, you should address it, introduce it, then ask it to be seated and get on with your presentation.

You have made contact with an audience when they perceive that you care and what you are saying benefits them. You have truly communicated when they decide to take action on that information.

As you prepare, consider the needs of your audience. At the very least, the subject must be of interest to them, or contain information that benefits them in some way. In any regard you must present it in such a manner that will capture their interest.

2. THE SUBJECT MUST BE WITHIN THE BOUNDS OF YOUR KNOWLEDGE.

When evaluating any potential subject, I ask myself two critical questions.

Do you know what you are talking about?

Shortly after I began my public speaking career, I was asked to speak to the sales force of a well-known company in Florida. I knew little about sales. My background was with faith-based organizations, and in those years teenagers made up the bulk of my audiences. In preparation I read two books by men who had made a profound influence on my life: *See You at the Top* by Zig Ziglar and *Life Is Tremendous* by Charlie "Tremendous" Jones. At that time in my life I didn't know what plagiarism was, but I was about to practice it in full form. I prepared a presentation about a subject I knew nothing about, repeating the words that these great men had written.

The speech went quite well until my host asked me to come to the front to answer questions. I was busted. My ignorance was on full display. It was one of the most embarrassing moments of my life. I should have spent more time studying the subject, asked to speak on a more familiar subject, or graciously declined the invitation.

In actuality this group didn't invite me as a sales expert. They wanted the kind of presentation I was known for—one filled with humor, encouragement, and motivation. When I stepped beyond the bounds of what I really knew, I let them down. The more intimately you know your subject, and are passionate about that subject, the more enthusiastic and genuine your presentation will be and the better it will be received.

Do you live what you are talking about?

The one ingredient that will bring passion to any presentation is the unshakable commitment of the speaker to the truth being presented. The enthusiasm of a salesperson who believes in his product gives him a persuasive edge that can never be duplicated in a canned sales talk. That is why many advertisers will only use spokespersons who have actually benefitted from using their product. When you are a living example of what you say, your message takes on a whole new level of effectiveness.

At a trade show in Las Vegas I had occasion to observe two people demonstrate a food processor. I saw the first person do the demonstration just as I entered the building. His sales patter was filled with humor, and he made good use of audience participation. Although the demonstration was interesting, several people, including me, drifted away about halfway through.

I wouldn't have given it another thought if I hadn't passed this same spot on my way out of the building. A new person was doing the demonstration and this person held the entire crowd, including me, until the very end. I waited while he filled several orders because I wanted to congratulate him on his presentation.

He had used the same sales talk, but something about his added enthusiasm and a sparkle in his eye made all the difference in the world. As we talked, I discovered the reason for his excitement. He was the inventor of the processor and owner of the company. The first person who gave the presentation was only doing his job, but the inventor believed in his product and enjoyed showing others how it worked.

That same kind of passion shows through when you present. If you believe in what you are talking about and care about the people you are sharing it with, the audience will know.

We've all had the experience of listening to speakers who were like these two salesmen. Some just seem to be "doing their jobs." What a difference it makes to sit at the feet of someone who is excited about their message!

Think Tony Robins, Billy Graham, Zig Ziglar, Seth Godin, or Michael Hyatt. These professionals hold our attention, and even when we disagree we listen because we know they believe passionately in what they are saying and care about how it affects the quality of our lives.

3. THE SUBJECT MAY BE LIMITED BY ASSIGNMENT.

Sometimes a speaker doesn't have the advantage of choosing a familiar subject. Teachers often have a lesson plan, corporate leadership limit their talks to meet the specific needs of their company, or a supervisor may dictate the subject. As a guest speaker you may be asked to deliver a speech on a special topic. Choose your subject accordingly.

C = CENTRAL THEME

Step two in the focusing process is to choose a single aspect of your subject as a central theme. The central theme must be brief and crystal clear. The purpose for choosing a central theme is to narrow the content of the talk to a manageable amount of specific information. This keeps the speaker from covering too much and keeps the audience from going into a coma. This narrowing process will make your talk more interesting and relevant.

Using one of the subjects mentioned above, here are examples of central themes you could develop.

SCUBA DIVING
- The thrills of scuba diving
- The dangers of scuba diving
- How to scuba dive safely
- How to learn to scuba dive
- How to make money scuba diving

Even though the subject of scuba diving seems narrow to start with, each of these central themes represents a separate aspect of scuba diving that more concisely defines a presentation.

Some are narrower than others, and any one of them would be more powerful than a speech that tried to cover the entire subject.

If you plan to talk about how to ride a horse, "horseback riding" is your subject. Your central theme would be a single aspect of horseback riding such as "How to ride a horse." "How to ride a horse safely" would narrow the central theme even more, and "How to most enjoy riding a horse" would be another talk altogether.

Sales might be your subject, but your central theme could range from "How to increase sales," to "How to maximize each sales opportunity," to "How to close sales," to "How to generate sales leads." All the confusion and much of the fear begins to drop away when a speaker narrows the focus of her talk ahead of time and knows exactly where she is headed.

Just as in sales, a narrow market is much easier to reach effectively than a broad one. It might be possible to give a general talk on all aspects of scuba diving, although I wouldn't recommend it unless your audience can hold their breath for a day or two. However, the subject of "social media" is so broad that entire books have been written about it and industries built around it. This book does not have space to list all the possible central themes on which this subject could be focused. The subject of social media is far too broad for a single speech, yet I have heard dozens of unfocused attempts to do just that. Often it was obvious that the speaker really wanted to emphasize a single aspect of the subject, but the lack of thoughtful preparation and no conscious effort to limit the presentation to a single objective made the temptation to ramble irresistible. These speakers wandered because they had not disciplined themselves to decide on their focus by choosing a single aspect of their subject as a central theme. Instead they reached deep into the barrel of information labeled "Social Media," grabbed an armload of material, and dumped it on the audience. Here are just a few of the possible central themes you could develop from the subject of social media:

- How to use social media to generate cash
- How to mine social media for prospects
- How to use social media to get your message to the world

- How to control personal time spent on social media
- Learning the basics of social media

Michael Hyatt, former chairman and CEO of Thomas Nelson Publishing, wrote a book entitled *Platform: How to Get Noticed in a Noisy World*. A substantial portion of the book deals with social media. How could one even hope to rationally cover the entire subject in a twenty-minute talk?

The process of choosing a central theme may lead you to reconsider your choice of a subject. For example, Bill, one of our SCORRE Conference students, chose "vacationing" as his subject. As he worked toward developing his central theme, it became obvious that he wanted to talk about the thrills of scuba diving. Thrills that he had discovered while on vacation. (Now you know where all that scuba diving talk came from.)

Once his focus was clear, he realized that his talk really had little to do with vacationing. He wasn't going to give any information on how to choose a vacation or why vacationing is important. He simply wanted to share the thrills of a specific vacation hobby—scuba diving. The process of narrowing his subject to a central theme clarified his own thoughts and kept him from straying. Be open to this kind of refinement until all the elements of your talk are crystal clear.

Just like Bill, as you define your objective and rationale you may find it necessary to go back again and adjust the subject and central theme to express your focus more accurately.

Examples of possible central themes with their corresponding subjects:	
SUCCESS	**LOVE**
Definitions of success	The joy of love
How to succeed	The need for love
The cost of success	The cost of love
Leveraging success	How to love
	The different kinds of love

FEAR	SUFFERING
Overcoming fear	Enduring suffering
Imagined fears	Understanding suffering
Facing fear	Causes of suffering
Identifying real fear	Positive results of suffering

FAITH	GROWTH
Roadblocks to faith	Obstacles to growth
Attitudes of faith	Steps to growth
The power of faith	Benefits of growth
The benefits of faith	Problems with growth
	Finding courage for growth

COMMUNICATION	BELIEFS
The demands of communication	Unfounded beliefs
Styles of communication	Integrated beliefs
The essentials of effective communication	Effects of belief on behavior
How to communicate with confidence	Changing beliefs
	Basic beliefs

RELATIONSHIPS	EDUCATION
Building relationships	Benefits of education
Family relationships	History of education
Healing broken relationships	
Adolescent relationships	
Workplace relationships	

REVIEW

After the following short review, use the space provided to write down a subject and central theme for the talk you will prepare using the SCORRE method. Take time to do this before you move on to the next chapter. The examples of central themes on page 27 may help you. Remember, the central theme will not necessarily express the objective of your talk. It will, however, represent what you are planning to talk about.

1. There are four basic guidelines to choosing a subject. The first is that the subject must touch the audience. It should meet a specific _____ of the audience or be of _____ to the audience.

2. The subject must be within the bounds of your _____.

3. The subject may be limited by _____.

4. Narrowing your focus to a central theme keeps you from trying to cover _____ _____.

5. The subject and central theme may not necessarily express the exact objective of your talk, but it will represent what you plan to _____ _____.

Now choose a subject and central theme. Do not be discouraged if you have difficulty narrowing your subject to a central theme. This is not in cement! What you learn in the next pages will clarify this process immensely and may motivate you to make changes to what you write here.

Although the process is not always easy, you will see the fruit of your efforts in clear and powerful presentations. Be brief and clear.

The subject for my talk is _____.
Write your previously chosen subject here or choose a new one.

The one aspect of that subject that I am choosing as a central theme is

_____.

Answers: 1. need, interest 2. knowledge 3. assignment 4. too much information 5. too much 6. talk about

Focusing in on the Objective

Identifying the Bull's-Eye

The most brilliant and helpful book I have ever read on the topic of speaking was written by a professor who lived almost a hundred years ago, J. H. Jowett. He lectured on preaching at Yale University, and his writings are profound insights for anyone who wants to communicate. He made the following statement concerning sermons. Its truth is applicable to the crafting of any talk. The italic additions are mine.

> I have a conviction that no sermon [*or talk*] is ready for preaching [*or being presented*], not ready for writing out, until we can express its theme in a short, pregnant sentence as clear as a crystal. I find the getting of that sentence is the hardest, the most exacting, and the most fruitful labour in my study.[1]

This is it! This is the final expression of that pinpoint of focus. It's where the rubber meets the road, where the buck finally stops. It all should be expressed in the construction of a single clear sentence. A sentence that identifies the objective of the talk.

As Jowett says, "the getting of that sentence is the hardest [remember that when you are tempted to put this book down and give up] . . . and the most fruitful [remember that as you decide to press on] labour in my study."

Diligence in preparation results in excellence on the platform.

Students of our SCORRE Conference are required to prepare and deliver several five-minute speeches. Occasionally someone will balk at the time limit. They ask, "How can delivering a five-minute speech apply to the real world where I regularly speak for twenty or thirty minutes?"

Diligence in preparation results in excellence on the platform.

Write the following sentence down! Frame it! Put in on your office wall!

If you can't say it in five minutes, you won't be able to say it in any amount of time available. I would go even further and agree with Mr. Jowett.

If you can't express the objective of your talk in a single sentence, you are not yet clear enough or focused enough to deliver it in any amount of time.

It is the process of writing this sentence that forces you to a powerful, focused objective. Learning that difficult but invaluable skill will be the subject of the next chapter. So put the book down, grab a cup of coffee, and with the enthusiasm of a professional communicator, tell someone, "I'm going to learn to write a sentence!"

Don't be ashamed of your enthusiasm. This is a sentence that will change the dynamics of your communication and perhaps the dynamics of your life.

If you can't say it in five minutes, you won't be able
to say it in any amount of time available.

This process is like great medicine. It is of absolutely no use unless you take it. It's like the lessons your golf pro might teach you. The only way you benefit from them is to practice. As in golf your SCORRE might suffer for a little while until the new process becomes natural. I often tell our SCORRE students that what they are about to learn will either help them or haunt them. Once you see what focused communication looks like, you will never be satisfied with less. You will listen to other speakers with a new ear. You will never be comfortable with mediocre speaking again. Commit to apply this to your preparation and watch what happens to the quality of your presentations and the response of your listeners.

O = OBJECTIVE

In this chapter I will list the steps for writing the all-important objective sentence. Though it may seem daunting to see the list of steps required, be patient because we will deconstruct the process and go over each of those steps in detail.

As you read I want to remind you again of this important truth.

The objective sentence determines the purpose and structure of your talk. However, it is not written in the same language or style you will use to deliver the talk. It is a map, a foundation, a plan—like the two-by-fours that frame a home and provide structure, but which the owners of the house never see. The means of accomplishing the plan can be as varied, creative, and unique as the people who execute it. Take another gulp of caffeine and let's get at it.

The objective sentence contains a proposition, an implied interrogative question (either how or why), and an interrogative response (answer to the how or why). This sentence will also contain a very important key word.

The objective sentence identifies the purpose of your presentation and indicates how you will accomplish that purpose. It will always look something like this:

- *Every person can be a more effective leader by applying four valuable leadership principles with their team.*

Notice that the sentence contains a proposition ("Every person can be a more effective leader"), the implied interrogation is, how? and the interrogative response is "by applying four valuable leadership principles with their team"). The key word in this sentence is "principles."

An interrogative response is an answer to a question. This particular interrogative response answers the question implicit in the proposition: How can every person become a more effective leader? It also contains a key word. In this sentence the key word is "principles." Each of the points of this talk will be a principle that will empower the listener to become a more effective leader.

Remember Jowett's words. Finding the one sentence that describes your objective can be a difficult and exacting process. It's not just any old sentence pulled from thin air. It is specific and feels constricting. It is designed to force you to achieve that pinpoint focus. It may limit the amount of material you can cover, but it will only enhance the power of your message.

You will be tempted to modify the form of the sentence. Don't do it. It has been tested and proven to keep you on track.

The sentence is rarely pretty, but neither is the foundation of your house. This ugly little sentence will enable you to know exactly what you want to say and how you want to say it. Save pretty for when you deliver the speech.

One of our SCORRE students raised this objection: "Not all speeches need an objective. Sometimes a speech is given only to disseminate information."

I asked the student, "Why would the speaker want to give this information?"

Having an objective is essential to good communication.

There was a long silence as the student realized he was trapped. If he answered my question he would be stating the objective for giving the information. On the other hand, if there was no purpose or objective for giving the information then why waste time giving it? Hand it out in a memo.

Informational talks are rarely boring if the audience understands why the information is important to them. When the listener makes the connection between the information and the benefit it brings to them, communication is born. Take the time to articulate why what you're saying is important to your listeners. I wonder how the attitude of a high school student might change if she knows how the "information" she was being required to learn would benefit her. I wonder how the content of what we teach would change if we asked that same question of the information we have chosen to teach.

Having an objective is essential to good communication. So let's break it down and look at the steps necessary to write this sentence.

1. Write a proposition.
2. Interrogate the proposition with how or why.
3. Write a response to the interrogation.
4. Choose a key word.

Let's look at each of those steps in detail.

Reminder! Every word in the objective sentence is designed to keep you on track and focused on a single objective. Use the exact words indicated in the examples as you prepare your own speech. These are not necessarily the exact words you will use when you deliver the speech, but they will help you organize your speech properly.

1. WRITE A PROPOSITION

In the context of this book, a proposition is a proposal put forth for consideration or acceptance. It will comprise the first half of your objective sentence. The proposition identifies the objective of your speech and provides a powerful focus for the ingredients of your message. Whereas the subject and central theme express what you want to talk about, the proposition identifies why.

There are two kinds of propositions to choose from, either a persuasive proposition or an enabling proposition.

Any speech will fall into one of those two categories.

A PERSUASIVE PROPOSITION

If you are attempting to motivate the audience to a particular action or view, you will write a persuasive proposition. The exact form for writing a persuasive proposition is

- Every _____ should _____.

The first blank in the sentence is to help you identify your target audience. Knowing who you are aiming at is as important as knowing what you are aiming at. If your talk is addressed to leaders, or parents, or clients, know it. Write it in the blank. If you are speaking to a general audience, write the word *person* in the blank.

Notice that the persuasive proposition always uses the word *should*. Don't be afraid of this word. Almost without exception you will be telling your audience they "should" be doing something so they will either avoid consequences or receive some kind of benefit. In the actual delivery of the speech, you will rarely actually use the word *should*, but, in the preparation process, commit to using it in your persuasive proposition.

The second blank is where you express the actual proposition. Written below are some examples of persuasive propositions, including ones developed from the subjects and central themes discussed in the previous chapter.

- Every person should learn to ride a horse.
- Every person should consider the sport of scuba diving.
- Every senior should get a flu shot.
- Every speaker should pinpoint his or her objective.

AN ENABLING PROPOSITION

Usually informational or instructional speeches have enabling propositions. This is what you might think of as a "how to" speech.

The exact form for writing an enabling proposition is

- Every _____ can _____.

The blanks work the same way as in a persuasive speech. Again, the first blank identifies your audience, and the second blank is for your actual proposition.

The enabling proposition always uses the word *can*.

Now notice the different direction that an enabling speech will take with the same subjects used previously.

- Every person can learn to ride a horse.
- Every person can learn to scuba dive.
- Every senior can avoid the flu.
- Every speaker can learn how to pinpoint his or her objective.

These will be totally different talks than when using a persuasive proposition.

....

There is an old proverb that says, "The man who
chases two rabbits catches neither."

....

Chapter 1 of this book was persuasive in nature. It gave all the reasons why you should speak with focus. This chapter has an enabling focus. It shows you how you can prepare more-focused speeches.

There is a real temptation to include both enabling and persuasive objectives in the same speech (we call this giving two speeches), but each message should have only one focused objective. There is an old proverb that says, "The man who chases two rabbits catches neither."

The argument for more than one objective is based on the desire not to leave an audience hanging. If you use a persuasive speech to convince a client to take advantage of the service you provide, how could you leave the room without showing them how? You CAN show them how, but it does NOT require giving another speech. In sales they call it a close, a simple instruction on how they can take advantage of whatever it is you just persuaded them that they need. In chapter 6, "The Total Communication Picture," we will resolve this dilemma. For now, when you write the proposition for your message, be sure to choose only one focus, persuasive or enabling.

So how do you decide which proposition to use to present your ideas? The best way is to write one and see if it leads to the ideas you wanted to present. For example, assume that you want to encourage your audience to learn to speak Spanish. Either of the following propositions would work.

- Every person can learn Spanish.
- Every person should learn Spanish.

If you use the enabling proposition, it will lead to a speech on what steps need to be taken to learn Spanish. If, on the other hand, you feel you must convince the audience of the importance of learning Spanish, you would use the persuasive proposition.

When it comes time to write your proposition, it is important to avoid two temptations that can short-circuit your effort.

First, avoid the temptation to try to use some dramatic statement from your speech as a part of your proposition.

It is so important to remember that the words you will say in your speech may be different than the words you use to describe what you want to accomplish with what you say. It is very tempting to try to slip a favorite line from your presentation into the proposition. Save it for the speech.

A young pastor who attended SCORRE was preparing a message for an upcoming wedding. He wrote this as his proposition:

- Every married couple should avoid the pitfalls of marriage.

He had just read an article about the pitfalls of marriage and wanted to pass this information on to the couple he was going to marry. However, once he had written the proposition, he was stuck. No wonder! "The pitfalls of marriage" is a pretty grim subject for a bride and groom standing at the altar. This young man had confused a topic he wanted to address in his message with the purpose for his message.

A single question broke the log jam of confusion and helped him see his true objective. "Why do you want this young couple to know about the pitfalls of marriage?" I asked.

Without hesitation he responded, "Because I want them to have a successful marriage."

His eyes lit up as he realized he had just stated his real objective. He wanted to help Bill and Mary have a successful marriage. It became obvious that the purpose of his message was going to be broader and much more positive than just a revelation of the pitfalls of marriage. Further questioning revealed that his message was composed of several guidelines that lead to a successful marriage. Avoiding the pitfalls that destroy marriage was only one of those guidelines. But because this one was burning a hole in his heart, it had found its way to the proposition where it didn't belong. His final proposition looked like this:

- Every couple (Bill and Mary) can increase their chances of having a successful marriage.

How? By following three simple guidelines. Avoiding the pitfalls that destroy marriage was one of those guidelines.

The proposition expresses the purpose of the message, not its actual content.

Second, avoid the temptation to change the basic structure of the sentence. Don't do it. The flexibility you desire will be fully available once you determine the objective for your talk. This temptation is usually a sign that you are trying to include the entire contents of your speech in the proposition. One more time: The proposition expresses the purpose of the message, not its actual content.

Here's a helpful hint. Read your proposition out loud and then ask the appropriate how or why question out loud! If you have the right proposition, there should be an explosion of rhetoric that follows. But if you suddenly seem trapped and aren't sure how to answer the question, one of two possible problems is true:

1. You have the wrong proposition.
2. You don't know enough about the subject to give a speech.

Using one of the formats below, write a proposition that expresses the objective of your talk. Be bold. Don't worry about making a mistake. You may come back later and adjust your proposition to express your objective more accurately.

If your speech is going to be persuasive, use this format:

- Every _____ should _____.

If your speech is going to be a "how to" enabling speech use this format:

- Every _____ can _____.

2. INTERROGATE THE PROPOSITION

Now that you have written a proposition using one of the formats provided, interrogate it with either the question how or why. The answer to that question will then be the second half of your objective sentence: the interrogatory response. Persuasive propositions always lead to the question, why? Enabling propositions lead to the question, how?

Interrogate your propositions out loud. The answer to the how or why question should lead to the content of your speech. If you are left with a blank and don't know how to answer, then you probably have the wrong proposition or you really don't have enough information to give the speech.

The young pastor who was preparing to preach at the wedding knew he wanted to give his friends guidelines that would help them in their marriage. Yet when he wrote the wrong proposition—"Every couple should avoid the pitfalls of marriage"—it did not lead him to the message that was brewing in his heart. If you interrogate his proposition with the question "why?" the only answer is, "so that they will have a successful marriage." This is a statement, not a speech. It did not lead this student to what he really wanted to say. However, when he correctly identified his proposition (Bill and Mary can have a successful marriage) and then interrogated it with the correct question (How?), he could hardly stop talking. He immediately began to list the guidelines that eventually became the body of his presentation. That is precisely what a good proposition does. It unleashes your talk.

Keep in mind that it is always easier to identify what we want to talk about than it is to identify the purpose of the talk. That is why writing a clear proposition is so difficult and yet so important. Here are some examples of different propositions developed from the same subject. Interrogate each proposition with how or why and draw a line from the proposition to the potential message on the right that most likely fits that proposition.

Potential propositions	Potential messages
1. **Persuasive** Every leader should develop listening skills	a. A talk that shows leader the benefits of learning to listen
2. **Enabling** Every leader can learn to listen	b. A talk that teaches conflict resolution skills
3. **Persuasive** Every person should take a college level course each year	c. A talk that details the benefits of continuing education
4. **Persuasive** Every person should learn to deal with conflict	d. A speech that might list the consequences of not facing conflict
5. **Enabling** Every person can learn to deal with conflict	e. A talk that shows leaders how to develop their listening skills
Answers: 1. a 2. e 3. c 4. d 5. b	

If what you have learned motivates you to change the wording of the proposition for the speech you are preparing, rewrite your proposition here. Stay relaxed. As you continue to learn more about developing this objective sentence, you can always come back and make changes.

• Every _____ should/can _____.

3. WRITE AN INTERROGATIVE RESPONSE

Once you have interrogated your proposition, it's time to answer the how or why question and write the second half of the sentence, the interrogative response. This response is a prepositional phrase containing a key word. To keep you focused you should write the prepositional phrase in a specific form.

The response to a persuasive proposition should always begin with the words *because of*.

• Every _____ should _____ (because of) _____.
• Every person should learn conflict resolution skills *because of* the CONSEQUENCES of unresolved conflict.
• Every person should learn to ride a horse *because of* the therapeutic BENEFITS of the sport.

There is one exception to this rule. If your key word is "reasons," as it often will be, then your interrogative response should begin with the word *for*.

• Every person should try scuba diving *for* three reasons.

The response to an enabling proposition should always begin with the word *by*.

• Every _____ can _____ (by) _____.

- Every person can learn to resolve conflict *by* developing four important SKILLS.
- Every person can learn to ride a horse *by* following these INSTRUCTIONS.

4. CHOOSE A KEY WORD

Notice that I have put one word in each of the above responses in capital letters. Those are the key words. The key word is always a plural noun that describes the content of your talk. It is one of the most important words in your objective sentence, and should be repeated consistently in the delivery of your talk. Without a key word the objective degenerates into a statement rather than a proposition.

Consider this objective:

- Every salesperson can increase their personal income by selling more.

Hellooo!
Nice ten-second speech. You can sit down now.
This does not lead the audience to want more information. Now look at the following objective sentence and see the difference that a key word makes:

- Every salesperson can increase their personal income by practicing Smooth Willie's master sales TECHNIQUES.

The key word is "techniques" and it causes the audience to ask, "What are Smooth Willie's master sales techniques?" Because of the way the objective is worded, the speaker will be focused on revealing those techniques. Notice that the adjectives preceding the key word give it even more definition and focus. This speech will not be about just any sales techniques. These are "master" techniques developed by Smooth Willie.

Suppose the speaker handed out a new manual that contains new techniques. He might then construct an objective sentence that looked like this:

Every salesperson can increase his personal income by practicing the new sales techniques found in our new manual.

The key word "techniques" causes the sales force to ask, "What new techniques in the manual?"

Always include a key word! And use the key word throughout your speech to keep your audience aware of where you are in the talk.

Three rules should govern your choice of a key word:

1. It must be a plural noun.
2. It should be as memorable as possible.
3. It must be a word that describes all the rationale (points) of your speech.

A corollary to the second rule is that, as much as possible, you should avoid using nondescript words like *ways*, *things*, or *stuff* as key words. "Things" are monsters that lurk in your closet. "Stuff" is that nastiness on the end of your son's finger. They are weak, lazy words. And in most cases, they can be easily replaced with a much more picturesque, powerful descriptive word.

My friend Jim Green who helped develop the SCORRE process had an English teacher who would fail any paper that contained the word *things*. She explained, "If you tell me to go up on the mountain where there are trees and things, I refuse to budge until I find out what the 'things' are." She is right. Those things could be innocent rocks or a band of marauding zombies. The reader or listener will never know, unless you use a word that describes what the "things" are.

There may be occasional times to use these words, but most of the time we use them because we are too lazy to think of a more descriptive, powerful key word. Look at the list of sample key words in the Appendix. Any one of them could be replaced with words like *things*, *stuff*, and *ways*. But their descriptive power would be lost in the process. So might the interest of your audience.

The key word is like a bag that holds the logical rationale of your speech together. Each of the points of your speech rationale will be derivatives of the key word. For instance, if your key word is *commands*, then each of the points in your speech will be a command.

Consider the following objective sentence:

> Every person should try scuba diving because of the THRILLS associated with this sport.

Every point in your speech will detail one of the thrills associated with the sport of scuba diving. You don't have to list them by number or make your speech sound academic and predictable. You might tell several stories, each one detailing a different thrill associated with the sport.

Consider this objective sentence I used to help me write my book *Fully Alive*:

- Every person can rediscover the joy in life by taking the STEPS to living fully alive.

Every chapter in the book details steps that will lead to finding joy in life again.

A properly chosen key word will make your speech more focused, easier to understand, easier to follow, and easier to remember. A list of example key words can be found in the Appendix section of this book.

As you can see from the list of key words, not all plural nouns end in *s*. The words *evidence* and *advice* are just two examples. In the beginning stick with those that do end in *s*. *Pieces* of evidence and *nuggets* of advice would still lead you in the right direction.

Once you have constructed a sentence by writing a proposition, interrogating the proposition with how or why, giving an interrogative response, and choosing a key word, that sentence is your objective. Coming up with that sentence will be the most difficult and most important part of your preparation.

If you wish to try to write an objective sentence using the subject and central theme you developed earlier, use the four steps to do so now. However, do not be discouraged if you find it difficult or seem to run into a brick wall. Eventually, you will begin to see how it all fits together.

You may find it helpful to read the next chapter on rationale and then come back to work on your objective sentence. Although it is imperative to write these instructions in a linear fashion, the actual construction of an objective sentence will take you back and forth through the entire process, refining each of the elements as they are affected by clarity in the other elements of construction.

REVIEW

Identify the plural noun that serves as the key word in each objective and circle it.

1. Every leader can build an enthusiastic team by implementing three strategies.
2. Every person should exercise regularly because of the benefits.
3. Every parent can motivate his child to clean their room by utilizing four incentives.
4. Every driver should avoid texting while driving because of the possible consequences.
5. Every person can learn to love reading by following these reading guidelines.

Answers: 1. Strategies 2. Benefits 3. Incentives 4. Consequences 5. Guidelines

In a moment, I'm going to ask you to write your own clear and focused objective sentence. But first, review the following to make sure you have a solid understanding of the objective-writing process.

1. What are the two kinds of propositions?

   a. _____ b._____

2. What are the four steps to writing an objective sentence?

   Step A: Write a _____.

   Step B: _____ the proposition with how or why.

   Step C: Write a _____ to the interrogation.

   Step D: Choose a _____ word.

3. Persuasive propositions are always interrogated with the word

   _____.

4. Enabling propositions are always interrogated with

   _____.

5. The interrogative response is a prepositional phrase containing a

   _____ word.

6. The response to a persuasive proposition should always begin with

   the words _____ _____.

7. The response to an enabling proposition should always begin with

   the word _____.

8. The key word is always a plural _____.

9. When you have constructed a sentence that contains a proposition,

   an interrogative response, and a key word, that sentence is your

   _____.

10. Now, take a few minutes to write an objective for a presentation you'd

   like to give. Double-check your work with the review above.

Answers: 1. a. persuasive b. enabling 2. Step A: proposition; Step B: interrogate; Step C: response; Step D: key; 3. why 4. how 5. key 6. because of 7. by 8. noun 9. objective

Developing Solid Rationale and Resources
That Makes Sense

When using the SCORRE process, everything gets more focused until you have written your objective. That is the pinpointed focus you have worked so hard to achieve. With that solid foundation established, the process reverses itself as you move outward and build a speech consisting of a broad base of rationale to support your objective.

R = RATIONALE

The fourth step in preparing a speech is to develop compelling rationale and the resources to support them. The rationale, more commonly known as the main points of the speech, establishes a logical foundation upon which the credibility of your speech will rest. If the key word is the bag that will hold all the elements of the talk together, then the rationale is the contents of the bag.

There are three rules that will govern your choice of rationale.

1. The rationale must correspond to the key word.

This is the first and most important rule of rationale. Consider using the following objective statement for your speech:

Every manager should require regular reports from tech support because of beneficial ideas that can be generated from the information.

- Ideas to improve product design
- Ideas to improve customer service
- Ideas to improve marketing strategy

This entire talk would be to persuade the managers to survey tech support. Why? Because of the beneficial ideas that could be generated from examining those reports. Each of the points of this talk would expand one of the possible beneficial ideas that might be found in that information. Can you see how this keeps all the elements of your talk related to the proposition? Everything you say will be the explanation or expansion of a beneficial idea that can be found in tech support data. And why are you revealing these hidden benefits? To encourage your managers to require the reports.

If you wanted to broaden the scope of rationale, you could use *reasons* as a key word:

- Every manager should require regular reports from tech support for three important reasons.

    1. They generate beneficial ideas.
    2. They promote a sense of teamwork
    3. They help clarify product branding.

In this scenario, what was once the core of an entire speech—"beneficial ideas"—is now the first rationale of a broader presentation.

Adding a simple adjective will affect the rationale you choose. Each of the following objective sentences contains the same proposition and key word, but the different adjectives subtly change the rationale and, as a result, the direction of the speech.

- Every person should go scuba diving because of three health benefits.

- Every person should go scuba diving because of three environmental benefits.
- Every person should go scuba diving because of three educational benefits.

"Benefits" is the key word in each of the propositions. Each of the rationale must not only be a benefit, but also be the kind of benefit indicated by the adjective.

2. The rationale should be brief.

There is a real tendency to try to include all the words you will use in speech in the rationale. It is much more important that the rationale be short and memorable. In your presentation you will have plenty of time to build your initial presentation of the rationale.

3. The rationale should be parallel in grammatical form.

If the rationale is the logic that will lead the audience to the objective, then it is important that it be stated in a form that is easy to remember. Consider this example. The key word is *facts* and the rationale is as follows:

- Fact #1: It is rare.
- Fact #2: It is valuable.
- Fact #3: Handle it carefully.

The third rationale breaks two of the rules above. First, "Handle it carefully" does not correspond to the key word. It is not a fact. "Handle it carefully" may be an instruction, a directive, or a command, but it's not a fact.

Second, it is not written in the same grammatical form as the other two. This can be solved by changing the wording to: "It is fragile."

The person who wrote this rationale certainly planned to caution his listeners to handle the merchandise carefully. He gave in to the temptation to put that statement in his rationale. Under the heading "It is fragile," he can still give the instruction to handle it carefully and keep the main points of his speech memorable.

At first glance this rule may seem trivial, but there is good reason for it. The human mind looks for patterns and hooks to help with comprehension and memory. A similar grammatical pattern provides such a hook. If I gave a talk on facts you should know about handling antique china, and if I stated my rationale as originally listed above, you would have difficulty remembering the third rationale because it didn't fit with the others. You can even feel something is askew as you read through the three rationale.

The most talked about presentation I ever delivered was developed to enable men and women to live to their fullest potential by applying three principles to everyday life.

- Live with nothing to prove.
- Live with nothing to hide.
- Live with nothing to lose.

Thirty years later I still receive e-mail and Facebook messages from people who remember those principles and seek to live by them.

Not all rationale will fit easily into such neat three-word sentences. But make every effort to keep them short and parallel in form. It will be worth it. It is unreasonable to expect that the audience will remember an entire speech. But if you state your rationale clearly and in a memorable way, people will remember the basics of your talk long after you have made your exit.

Remember that during the whole process of SCORRE you are looking for the best combination of ingredients to make your speech focused and clear. As you prepare the rationale for a speech, you might discover that the rationale you want to use doesn't fit your previously chosen key word. Simply go back and choose a more appropriate key word. For example, you might decide that the following rationale best fits your talk on handling precious china.

- Research its history.
- Know its value.
- Handle it carefully.

Your key word in this case might be steps or directions. It certainly wouldn't be *facts*. None of those rationales could be described as a fact.

When you have finally written your objective sentence and identified your rationale, you have the most basic outline necessary for any speech. Once you have learned the process, you can experiment with how you are most comfortable coming to this point. Exactly how you get there is not as important as the fact that you reach that crystal-clear focus. Imagine stepping to the platform with no doubt about what you want to accomplish and a detailed plan of how you are going to do it. That's confidence.

As I mentioned before, when I am preparing a talk, I usually write my objective sentence first. Then, once I have written my rationale I go back and make sure I have chosen the most powerful key word. No matter how you work the process, the final result should lead to that single objective you wish to achieve.

R = RESOURCES

When you have written your objective sentence and rationale, the fifth step in developing your speech is to add powerful resources. Now that the hard work is over, the fun begins. It's time to add the illustrations, data, anecdotes, and humor "resources" that will bring the talk to life.

As you choose which resources you are going to use, keep these facts in mind:

Resources should bring light, color, and clarification to your talk.

Denver, Colorado, has a beautiful City and County Building. Its Roman columns and stately architecture are remarkable. But for 335 days a year, thousands of people drive by this building and never give it a second glance.

At Christmas all of that changes. During the holiday season the city spends thousands of dollars lighting the building with magnificent colored floodlights. People travel hundreds of miles to see this gorgeous sight. The building doesn't change, but the lights draw attention and appreciation to what was there all along. The lights by themselves would draw little attention, but when they are focused on the structure, they make people notice what was previously ignored. That's how the resources such as illustrations work.

Resources should make the audience want to listen.

The human mind is capable of miraculous feats, but it is hard-pressed to concentrate for any extended period of time. The mind will tend to wander during a presentation unless it is held by the color and clarification of illustrations, humor, and supportive resources.

Resources should clarify and strengthen your rationale.

Sometimes the audience may question your proposition and the logic that led to it. Resources help you provide additional evidence to support your points.

Suppose you are trying to persuade your team to set goals for developing a healthier lifestyle in the coming year. You make the claim that personal good health results in a happier team. That's a nice thought, but it might not seem believable until you quote the statistics that back up your claim. When they learn that there is more beneficial serotonin released in the body from an hour of exercise in the sun than is allowed in any single dose of depression medicine, your words become more than opinion. This single fascinating fact may motivate someone to take your point seriously. If you can further support your rationale with the testimonial of a real person, the impact is even greater. Then both the statistics and your personal story become resources that strengthen your rationale.

Resources should never be an end in themselves.

Just because you've heard a great illustration is not reason enough to include it in your talk. Many times I have observed a speaker use up fifteen minutes of a twenty-minute talk telling a story that only marginally supported some minute point. (Many times I was that speaker.) When that happens, the real focus of the talk gets lost. As one who uses humor extensively, I often think of new illustrations even as I talk. There was a time I would include such a story just because it was funny. Now unless it helps my audience listen or lead them to the objective of the talk I won't even consider it.

Occasionally an illustration may be so emotionally charged that it distracts from the focus. One of my associates used to tell a true story from a book he had read that was so graphic and horrible that the audience couldn't get beyond it. It applied to the point he was trying to make, but the raw emotion it evoked distracted from the objective. People actually begged him to remove it from his presentation, which is a pretty good sign it was not helpful.

Never let the resources become an end in themselves.

REVIEW

Using the objective you wrote in the previous chapter exercise, take a few moments to work on a list of potential rationale to support your objective. Then, evaluate those rationales by answering the following questions:

1. Do my rationale correspond to the key word?
2. Are they brief?
3. Are they parallel in grammatical form?

Now consider potential resources for this presentation. Do you have quotes, stories, visual images, or other resources that would bring further clarity and focus to the message you want to convey? List potential resources below.

The Never-Ending Process of Evaluation

Reaching for Excellence

E = EVALUATION

The final step in preparing a speech is to evaluate your talk. The process of evaluation should be one that continues from the inception of a talk, through preparation and delivery, to long after you have left the platform and are assessing the effectiveness of your presentation. You should ask yourself the following questions repeatedly. They will also serve as a review of the material covered in this chapter.

- Do my subject, central theme, objective sentence, and rationale all fit together in an organized and logical manner?
- Do I have the right proposition?
- Have I interrogated my proposition properly?
- Is my response written properly, with clarity, and does it contain the best key word?
- Do the rationale match the key word, and are they brief and clear?
- Have I given the audience an opportunity for application or response to the message?
- Will this message meet the real needs of my audience?
- Do I know what I am talking about?

- Do I practice what I am talking about?
- Do I have enough information to speak with intelligence on the subject I have chosen?
- Do I really believe and live by the principles I am presenting?
- Am I excited about fleshing out this message and presenting it?

Continue to evaluate even the most carefully prepared message right through its presentation. In addition to the above questions, you might want to consider the following as well:

- What is the mood of my audience?
- What has happened in this community or group that has impacted them?

An effective communicator will massage the message to fit these variables.

As you give a talk to your associates on team building, a woman interrupts. "What I want to know is if the downsizing we have been hearing about is going to affect our jobs." Before you can respond she continues, "What good is it for us to talk about team building if we are not going to be a part of the team?"

Your originally planned talk will not be heard unless such an interruption is addressed. You might have to save your planned talk for another time and informally address the needs of this audience on the spot. It's all a part of evaluation.

On the Sunday following September 11, 2001, every good preacher in the country scrapped the prepared message and addressed the issue that was foremost in the mind of every person sitting in the congregation. Many didn't speak at all, but spent time praying for the country and its loss.

If someone died in the middle of your talk, you would not continue as though nothing happened. If a fire alarm went off, you would not insist that everyone sit tight until you are finished. Communication always takes into consideration the audience and the immediate environment. Evaluation of those considerations and using them to empower your message is the constant job of a great communicator.

Most last-minute evaluations affect the tone of your message, not its structure. When your reaction to an interruption demonstrates that you are aware of and care for your audience, it drives your message deeper than any authoritative lecture you might have planned.

Similarly, the humorous tone you planned for a speech may not be appropriate for an audience that has just gone through difficult circumstances. I once had a man have a heart attack during a presentation that was steeped in comedy. Evidently, laughter is not always good medicine. Several thousand people sat in silence as the EMTs stabilized him and took him out to the waiting ambulance. There is no way to continue such a meeting. We offered a refund to all who attended. Many people refused to accept a refund and we received messages of appreciation for our sensitivity to the moment. Coincidentally, the man later wrote to say it was his fifth heart attack, and the best heart attack he ever had.

REVIEW

Once you have a solid objective, supporting rationale, and potential resources to bring light and color to your talk, it's time to evaluate. Ask yourself the following questions. You'll do this multiple times before you present your message, as well as after:

1. Do my subject, central theme, objective sentence, and rationale all fit together in an organized and logical manner?
2. Do I have the right proposition?
3. Have I interrogated my proposition properly?
4. Is my response written properly, with clarity, and does it contain the best key word?
5. Do the rationales match the key word, and are they brief and clear?
6. Have I given the audience an opportunity for application or response to the message?
7. Will this message meet the real needs of my audience?
8. Do I know what I am talking about?
9. Do I practice what I am talking about?

10. Do I have enough information to speak with intelligence on the subject I have chosen?

11. Do I really believe and live by the principles I am presenting?

12. Am I excited about fleshing out this message and presenting it?

The Total Communication Picture

Putting It All Together

Once you have written your objective sentence, chosen a key word, and determined what your rationale are, write that information down on a piece of paper and draw a heart around it. From now on you will always think of the objective sentence and rationale as the heart of your presentation. It's the solid foundation from which the rest of your message builds. Once you have the framework, creativity can be set free to add your unique texture and color to your message.

This chapter helps you learn to think in outline form, by identifying the other parts of your presentation.

LEARN TO THINK IN OUTLINE FORM

When you *SCORRE* a speech by writing an objective sentence and rationale, that sentence and the rationale that supports it contain the focal point for everything that will happen from the time you step to the platform until you sit down. But you will actually say more than just what is contained in that skeletal structure.

The actual outline of your entire talk has three major parts. The first part is the opening, to prepare the audience to hear what you are going to say. The last part is the closing, to make your talk and your objective unforgettable. Sandwiched between is the heart of your message: SCORRE.

This outline has two important functions. First of all, it keeps you organized. Anything that does not lead to the objective of the speech will not fit well in the outline.

Second, it keeps you on time. If you use the blanks to the left of the outline (see example outline on the next page) to give each part of the speech a time value, it will help you prepare and deliver a balanced speech.

Many times I have labored over an important message, afraid that I might not have enough material, and then ended up running out of time on my first point. The fear of not having enough to say causes many speakers to prepare too much content. Once they are behind the podium, the adrenaline takes over and they wax eloquent on the introduction or first couple of points, only to realize too late that there is no time left to give the rest of the speech.

PUTTING IT ALL TOGETHER
30 Minutes: Four skills to better parenting

7:00pm

OPENING
5 minutes

ATTENTION GETTER *1 MINUTE*

    1 min. Story: Where did I come from?

INTRODUCTION: The need for better parenting *4 MINUTES*

    1 min. Other parents' frustrations
    1 min. Personal frustrations
    1 min. National Survey: 81% need help
    1 min. The shopping story

7:05pm

SCORRE
20 minutes

THE SOLUTION: Transition into objective of talk *1 MINUTE*

    1 min. We all want to be better parents. Tonight I would like to identify 4 skills that will help us achieve that goal.

1. Develop a sense of humor *5 MINUTES*
    1 min. A. Norman Cousins quote
    2 min. B. Third-grade teacher's example.
    2 min. C. Definition: Parallel to gospel message.

2. Develop a spirit of forgiveness *5 MINUTES*
    2 min. A. Survey: "I'm sorry. I was wrong."
    1 min. B. George Washington quote.
    2 min. C. Story. Teenage Prostitute

3. Develop an attitude of encouragement *3 MINUTES*
    2 min. A. Story: The gold miner.
    1 min. B. Personal illustration: H.S. teacher

4. Develop an atmosphere of trust *6 MINUTES*
    3 min. A. Trust your child. Expect the best.
    3 min. B. Trust God. He cares more than you do.

7:25pm

CLOSING
5 minutes

REVIEW: Objective and rationale *1 MINUTE*

APPLICATION: What steps will you take to develop these skills? Introduce "Family Feud" parenting class starting January 7. *3 MINUTES*

PRAYER: For strength to respond to God's leading. *1 MINUTE*

Although this outline means little to the casual reader, the phrases and words remind the well-prepared speaker of illustrations, quotes, and other points that flesh out the speech.

As you outline your speech, estimate how much time you have to spend on each element, then prepare the most convincing material to fill that allotment and stick to the limits you set for yourself. My friend C. McNair Wilson encourages our students to be OYFOL speakers. That means you should never deliver a speech without practicing it On Your Feet Out Loud. This is an invaluable step in preparation. It will give you a realistic idea of how much time each part of the presentation will take. Years of practice have taught me that when a presentation is actually delivered, it will take 10 to 20 percent longer than you think. Practicing out loud also helps identify areas where you may stumble and will greatly enhance the quality of your presentation. Some concepts and words are easy to think and almost impossible to say. You can think of rubber baby buggy bumpers without a problem, but just try saying it three times. I read every word of every book I write out loud. It helps me discover clumsy concepts and sloppy writing. It works just as well for speaking. Practicing out loud will immeasurably enhance the quality of your delivery.

Although this outline means little to the casual reader, the phrases and words remind the well-prepared OYFOL speaker of illustrations, quotes, and other points that flesh out the speech. There are three major parts to the outline.

1. THE OPENING

Use the opening of your speech to get the audience to want to hear what you are going to say. At this crucial juncture, they will decide whether they will listen to you or not. If your opening fails to grab their interest, chances are slim that you will win them back later.

You must make the audience understand why you want to talk to them and make them believe that it is worth their time to listen.

Before a farmer can plant a seed, he must prepare the soil to receive it. Before a speaker can communicate, he must break through the audience's "what have you got to say that is of interest to me?" attitude and take control. You must make the audience understand why you want to talk to them and make them believe that it is worth their time to listen. Each group you speak to will require a different approach. But, in general, you have multiple objectives to achieve with your opening:

- Establish connection with the audience.
- Stir interest in the subject.
- Show the basis for giving the talk.
- Develop rapport with the audience.
- Make the audience want to listen.
- Prepare the audience for what you will say.

THE ATTENTION-GETTER

The attention-getter is an important part of the opening because it lets you establish contact and take control.

The way you approach the platform will have a major effect on gaining the attention of your audience. Be confident. Approach the front with the attitude of a quarterback coming onto the football field. There is a job to be done and you are the one in charge.

The sense of command and confidence in your voice as you say "Good evening" can be all it takes to let the audience know that you want their attention, and an anecdote or humorous story delivered with enthusiasm may also help gain you a hearing. How different this is than the timid tap on the mike followed by the meek request, "May I please have your attention?" Or worse, the same tap followed by the question, "Is this on? Is this on?"

How much better to start with a question, the statement of a problem, or a story that sets up the audience to hear your presentation. "Research tells us that half of the people in this room will be penniless at the end of life. That research is wrong and I will prove it. (pause) All of you will be penniless." I heard this speech and can guarantee I was prepared to listen to this speaker.

If your demeanor and first words get the audience's attention, what follows must quickly convince them that you deserve that attention.

I recently asked our youth worker how he got the attention of his junior high students. "When they come into the room," he said, "they are so full of energy that they can hardly sit still. I have forty-five minutes of class time. We play wild games and use a lot of group dynamics for forty minutes. At the end of that time they are worn out just enough so that they stop for a breath of air. At that moment," he declared, "I have about ten minutes to drive home the heart of my message." He uses interactive games and discussion to prepare his young audience to hear what he has to say.

THE INTRODUCTION

The introduction should be designed to prepare your audience for the SCORRE'd content of your speech. It should make very clear what the focus of the message is going to be. No unrelated jokes or stories here. If a joke or story doesn't further the objection or stir the interest of the audience, it's unnecessary. A good introduction should stir interest in the content of your talk. At this point in the talk, what each member of the audience wants to know more than anything else is, "What is this talk going to be about and what does it have to do with me?" Too often the speaker doesn't ever give a clue.

Use the introduction to state your objective clearly and leave your audience eager for more.

If I stepped in front of a group of businesspeople in a large office building and began to describe three routes that would enable them to leave the building in less than one minute, chances are I would lose their attention almost immediately. Why would they care?

But suppose I step to the front and with authority say, "Ladies and gentlemen, there's a fire on the lower floors. The only way you can survive is to leave the building within sixty seconds. I will give you three routes you can take that will save your life."

With an introduction like that, the audience wants to know, "What routes?"

If I had to write an objective sentence for this speech, it would have looked like this:

• Every person can survive this fire by taking one of three routes.

But notice that while delivering the speech, I clearly stated the objective in conversational English.

Often I give a presentation entitled "How to Get the Most Out of Life." I quote a familiar beer commercial as an attention-getter. (That always works.) The commercial begins with the words: "You only go around once, so you've got to reach for all the gusto you can get." The commercial suggests that you can get all of the gusto out of life by drinking their beer. In my introduction I draw attention to the crafty wisdom of the advertiser in pointing out two truths. We really do only go around once, and most men and women I know want to live life with gusto. But beer won't bring any more gusto to your life than eating watermelon. So what will? As a transition to the content of my message I say, "There are three principles you can live by that will bring more gusto to your life than you ever dreamed possible."

Sometimes the attention-getter and the introduction are contained in the same phrase. Speaking to a church group I began with this sentence: "You can learn to hate God, and tonight I'll show you how." My talk was designed to show the attitudes that cause us to move away from God. I guarantee everyone was listening as I started.

Here is an overview of information relevant to a good opener in outline form:

Ingredients of a Good Opening
• An attention-getter
• An introduction
• A transition to the SCORRE'd message

Purpose of the Opening
• Establish contact with the listener (attention-getter)
• Develop positive rapport
• Stir interest in the text or topic
• Make the audience want to listen

Qualities of a Good Opening
- Brief
- Clear
- Appropriate
- Purposeful
- Audience-centered

Characteristics of a Poor Opening
- Full of flattery
- Apology-ridden
- Predictable
- Complex
- Without purpose

Options for a Good Opening
- Startling statement
- Question
- Quotation
- Humorous story
- Vivid word picture
- Comparison
- Discovery
- Statement of problem
- Visual aid
- Music
- Proposition*
- Prediction
- Reference to a current event
- Personal observation
- Dramatic presentation
- A joke
- Media
- A conundrum
- A paradox

- A Scripture reading
- Definition

*Your objective sentence (in conversational form) should be a part of every opener. As a proposition it serves very well as the transition to the heart of the message.

2. THE HEART OF THE SPEECH

This is the focused presentation you planned, using the SCORRE process. In its full outline form it will now include illustrations and data not included when you simply had an objective sentence and a list of rationale.

In the opening you catch the attention and interest of the audience. In the heart of the message you must deliver on accomplishing the objective. Everything you do and say before you get to the heart of the message should be designed to prepare the audience to hear it. Everything you will say in your conclusion will relate the objective you tried to drive home. The minute you lose sight of the singular focus and central importance of your objective, you will defuse your talk of its potential power.

3. THE CONCLUSION

There is a saying in show business: "You're only as good as your last performance." The same can be said for a speech. "You're only as good as the last words you say!" Millions of good speeches have been ruined by long, drawn-out, inconclusive endings. I cringe whenever I hear the words "and in conclusion," because many times it signals the beginning of another speech. I want to warn the speaker, "Land the plane! You're running out of fuel and the audience is running out of patience!"

The basic purpose of a conclusion is to summarize the rationale and objective of your talk, give opportunity for application or response, and burn the focus into the hearts and minds of the listeners. On the surface it may seem simplistic, but in practice it works.

A brief summary of the logic that led to your objective should be a part of every conclusion.

Using the conclusion to allow the audience to respond to a message solves a common frustration. If the speaker has convinced the audience of the need to take action, it is only proper that that same speaker give the audience opportunity to do so. This does not mean giving another speech, but rather using the concluding remarks to point your audience to a meaningful way to respond.

Imagine a salesperson spending an hour convincing her prospective client of the benefits of buying a widget. After her presentation the prospective client is so convinced of his need for the widget that he begins weeping. At that point the salesperson closes her presentation book and walks out the door. And the prospective client, now fully convinced he needs the widget, is left empty-handed.

In the same way, don't leave your audience's need unattended and unfulfilled. Show them where they can sign to gain the benefits you have promised.

Purpose of the Conclusion
- To restate the objective and remind the listener of the logic that led to that objective (should be part of every conclusion)
- To give opportunity for response or application
- To summarize the talk

Qualities of a Good Conclusion
- Brief
- Clear
- Unifying
- Well-prepared
- Appropriate
- Practical
- Memorable

Characteristics of a Poor Conclusion
- Long and drawn-out

- Unrelated to the message
- Weak and forgettable
- Without summary of rationale and proposition
- Another message

Optional Components of a Conclusion
- Restatement of rationale and objective
- Quotation
- Challenge
- Brief story or illustration
- Prayer
- Public response
- Suggested course of action
- Striking statement
- Appeal for consideration
- Suggested application
- Music
- Media
- Drama
- Personal story
- Contemplative silence

REVIEW

Consider your working objective and rationale. Brainstorm a possible opening and closing that would serve the purposes of both. Record your ideas here:

Finding, Filing, and Crafting Illustrations

Make It Shine

Congratulations! The hard part is over. Now the creative and fun part begins. Lets talk about illustrations. A good illustration has the power to lift an abstract idea to a position of interest and practical application. It can snap a wandering mind back to attention, convince a doubting mind of truth, and clarify a difficult concept.

You can enhance the dynamics of your communication by adopting the practices presented in this chapter for finding, filing, and crafting good illustrations.

Before you can use illustrations, you have to find them. This turns out to be easier than it sounds. The best illustrations are not found in some book entitled *2001 Great Illustrations*. The best illustrations are all around you. One of the most productive steps you can take to increase your effectiveness as a speaker is to learn how to recognize great illustrations that present themselves in everyday life. You can always supplement the real-life experiences you encounter with other valuable resources. And finally, you will need to develop a filing and retrieval system that helps you find these illustrations when you need them.

CAPTURING LIFE'S ILLUSTRATIONS

LOOK

Any person who writes or speaks needs to be constantly on the prowl for illustrations. Not just for the project you are working on now, but also for future speeches that have not even been developed yet. You need the eye of the hunter to recognize good illustrations when you see them. Most of us go through life with a kind of tunnel vision that causes us to pass up hundreds of potentially good illustrations every day.

Every time you go for a walk, read a book, listen to a speaker, or go to the supermarket, you are in prime hunting territory to gather excellent illustrations. But you have to know what to look for.

When I first started driving to Estes Park, Colorado, with our staff to do what we now call the SCORRE Conference, we would pass through some of the finest big game country in the world. Because I have hunted all my life, I have trained myself to be on the lookout for animals at all times. During this beautiful drive I would spot elk or deer standing in the forest near the road. I would jam on the brakes. The car would screech to a halt and I would spend the next fifteen minutes trying to get my staff to see what I had trained my eyes to see. "See the big rock about halfway up the mountain?" I would whisper, pointing frantically in the direction of the rock and the animal standing next to it. "Look just to the left of that big rock, under the tallest pine tree." Sometimes after physically holding their heads in the direction of the animal and sighting down the part in their hair I could get my friends to see what I saw. Over the years I taught my friends what to look for. Now they spot animals before I do.

Animals, like illustrations, seldom stand out in the open where they can be seen from head to tail. They are partially obscured by trees, bushes, and other vegetation. The hunter develops a sharp eye for the clues that will alert him to the presence of an animal. For example, horizontal lines are a clue. In the forest they are present in only two basic forms: the back of a large animal such as a deer or the line formed by a fallen tree. If you see a horizontal line seventy feet long, it's not likely to be a deer. However, every horizontal line is worth inspection because a certain percentage of them end up having legs and horns.

The color white is another clue. In the summer, the color white is seldom found in Colorado forests except on the rump of an animal. Close investigation of a small patch of white will often reveal the partially hidden body of an elk or deer. Any patch of white is worth investigating.

Black buttons are another clue. In the winter rabbits turn white and are perfectly camouflaged against the snow. But their eyes don't turn white. Many times I have stared for long minutes at a round black button in the brush only a few feet from where I stood. I couldn't see a rabbit, only the button. As I stepped forward for a closer look, the button would bounce away, now connected to the totally visible body of a bunny.

The illustrations we encounter in everyday life are like those animals hidden in the forest. They are partially hidden by our preoccupation and the circumstances that surround them. Because we aren't looking we miss them. We don't think of them as good illustrations because they don't seem dramatic enough. Yet it is this very camouflaging connection with everyday life that makes them real and powerful. Here is an example.

On a long and tiring flight a small child was running up and down the aisles. Although she was a beautiful child, her unsupervised shenanigans were disturbing several passengers. This all came to an abrupt halt when she crawled over an empty seat and fell into the lap of a passenger, putting a bruise on his head in the process.

The passenger called a flight attendant, who quickly brought the child to her mother and instructed her to keep the girl in her seat. The mother sat the child down, pulled the seat belt tight across her lap, and ordered, "Now you sit still." The girl sat absolutely still, but she had a huge, mischievous grin on her face.

"Why are you smiling?" the mother snapped.

"Because," the little girl smirked, arms folded across her chest, "I may be sitting on the outside, but on the inside I'm still running around."

This would be the perfect illustration for a speech on working with teenagers. Many times we restrain the outside behavior without considering what is on the inside. Whether we are trying to teach children proper behavior or communicating expectations to a team of coworkers, we can rest assured they will be dutifully obedient as long as the seat belt is tight. Yet if we do nothing to affect their inner attitudes, the instant the seat belt is released, or when no one is looking, whatever attitude exists on the inside will express itself in outward behavior. What may have seemed like genuine loyalty or commitment will be recognized as only outward compliance. The person who is running around on the inside will eventually run around on the outside.

Stories are the treasured currency of communication.

Train yourself to look for the telltale clues that indicate there might be an illustration hiding nearby. Discipline yourself to look for the signs. Don't allow people and events around you to slip by unnoticed. Become an observer. Learn to watch people. You will find a rich source of illustrations that you once passed by without even a glance. If you are a public speaker or writer, your radar should be fine-tuned to use every source at your disposal, to keep your eyes open every minute of the day for those experiences and stories that will make your talks unforgettable.

Stories are the treasured currency of communication. Careful observation of human behavior will reveal more illustrations than you can possibly use.

During a trip to Disneyland, as we entered the park I watched a young mother dressed in a bright pink dress escorting her small boy into the park. "Today we are going to see a big duck and a big mouse and go on some fun rides," she bubbled as they faded into the crowd. I spotted her pink dress again at the end of the day as we were leaving the park. It had been about ninety-five degrees all day, and the park was saturated with sweaty people. Some rides required more than an hour's wait in line. After eight hours Pink Mommy had the same energetic little boy by the same arm. But this time she was jerking him along giving him gruff details about what his father was going to do to him when he got home. I'm sure this mother loved her little boy. But her attitude had been severely affected by the temperature, the crowds, and two very sore feet.

I have used this illustration on several occasions to show how quickly we can allow circumstances to control our attitude rather than allowing our attitude to control how we face circumstances. We can't choose circumstances, but we can choose our attitude. These stories are currency, like a penny on the ground. If you're not looking for it, you'll walk right past it. Learn to look for it.

What are the telltale signs to look for? Quite simply it boils down to this: anything that moves you emotionally has the potential to be a powerful illustration. If something catches your attention, if it makes you laugh or cry or want to scream, it has the potential to do the same for your listener. If an event in your everyday life has that effect on you, chances are it will have the same effect on an audience. Anything out of the ordinary should snap you to full attention. That rude driver who cut you off in traffic, the little boy who asks a bizarre question, the story in the newspaper of the cat who followed a family after they moved five hundred miles away, a powerful blog, a poignant line in a motion picture—all these can provide excellent possibilities for adding light and color to your talks.

YouTube clips and other Internet resources can also be a rich source of illustration. A word of caution, however. The Internet is infected with many stories that are not true. No matter what your source, it is critical to verify, verify, verify. For one of my books I quoted a newspaper article about a reunion between a Vietnam vet and a woman from the village he had bombed. Fortunately I had a good editor. He checked the story only to find that the soldier had made it all up. So be sure you double-check your sources.

READ

The best speakers are voracious readers. Reading is like priming the pump. If we only rely on our own imagined creativity and genius, we will soon be out of material and out of work. Creativity is really at its peak when we are stimulated by the thoughts and work of others. Books are a vital resource for illustrations. Being well read is a quality that can separate a great communicator from a mediocre one and brings credibility and depth to any presentation. Charlie "Tremendous" Jones always said, "Five years from today, you will be the same person that you are today, except for the books you read and the people you meet." I would not hesitate to claim that books and people are also the two richest resources for illustrations.

Subscribe to magazines, blogs, and other resources that will keep you informed and relevant in your area of expertise. Know what is happening in current events around the world. Look at every medium of communication as a resource for illustrations. Here is a partial list of areas that should be conscious hunting grounds.

- Books
- Television
- Movies
- Magazines
- Websites/blogs
- YouTube
- Newspapers
- Podcasts
- Family life
- Radio
- Facebook
- Twitter

Years ago while preparing one of my talks I stumbled across an article in *Time* about Dan Jansen, the speed skater who fell twice in the 1988 Winter Olympics. His sister had died of cancer just hours before his first race. *Time* recorded the sad drama that ended years of sacrifice and physical preparation.

It was an anxious and grieving Jansen on the starting line that evening. At the outset he jumped the gun. To avoid a repeat and disqualification, he held back for a crucial moment at the second gun, then bore down to make up for lost time. He went down suddenly in the first turn . . . then he fell the second time, on the straightaway of Thursday's 1,000-meter event, just 200 meters short of the finish. It was even more stunning, as if he had been forced down by sorrow alone. Watching from the Gallery, brother Mike, 24, had just assured a sister: "Dan's made it through the toughest turns. He's fine now." At the 600-meter mark, Janzen was .31 seconds faster than any of the competition, then his right skate "caught an edge"—hit the ice on the side instead of the bottom of the blade—sending him to his hands and knees and into a wall. For a moment he sat on the ice, unbelieving, until Coach Mike Crowe and teammate Nick Thometz came over to help him off. Arriving at the bench area, he embraced his fiancee, Canadian speed skater Natalie Grenier, and sobbed.[1]

Why would this strike me as an illustration? Because so many people can identify with that hopeless feeling that accompanies an apparent failure. Because I was reading with one eye looking for illustrations, I realized that others would also feel the emotion and inspiration I felt upon reading this story. I would use this to talk later about how even in the most hopeless moments, we can lean on faith and friends to give us a new start. In fact, Dan Jensen did not give up. He would miss other opportunities to medal and fall in still another race, but eventually in 1994 Dan won a gold medal in the 1000-meter race. To this day his story serves as inspiration to many who have come on hard times.

If I hadn't taken the time to read *Time* magazine, I would've missed Dan's story and a powerful illustration that strengthened my presentation.

I subscribe to as many books and magazines online as possible. This makes the process of filing away any worthy illustrations I find as easy as "copy and paste." But when you do find an illustration in an actual magazine (remember those?) or in other written form, there is no need to retype it. Tear the article from the magazine, file it as a hard copy, and reference the general gist of the article in your digital folder along with where you can find it in your hard files.

Remember to credit speakers, publications, and authors you quote. File reference data along with any quote or copywritten material you save. Your credibility is at stake. Doing so also gives the audience a chance to research your topic in more detail.

Signs and bumper stickers will often provide a resource of illustrations. One of the most poignant bumper stickers I have encountered was "Don't follow me—I'm lost." It was designed to be funny but also provided a powerful point on choosing carefully who we follow.

Sometimes a quote or casual remark will provide an illustration that drives your point home. I frequently lecture on the importance of humor in everyday life. A remark attributed to Victor Borge provided a perfect highlight for my view of the value of humor. Borge is reported to have said, "Humor is the shortest distance between two people."

By now nearly everyone has heard of the little girl who misquoted the Twenty-third Psalm. When asked to recite, she stood with prim confidence and declared, "The Lord is my shepherd and that's all I want." That will preach!

JOURNAL

One of the best ways to keep ideas coming and keep a fresh and positive outlook on life is to keep a daily journal of your life. Your own thoughts, moods, successes, and failures will give you the foundation for many excellent illustrations. But it is not wise to use only your own experiences as a resource. If people only hear stories about your life, it can start to feel kind of shallow. Using the quotes and stories of others adds credibility and depth. Your stories are important. There are times when stories of your personal struggles and journey will breathe life into the message you are giving. They take on even more value when mixed with stories that reflect the fact that you are reading and doing research for your presentation.

Keep a digital journal of your discoveries, your challenges, and things to be grateful for. If they are of illustration status, file them under the proper topic. Think through the topics your thoughts or stories might be filed under and get them recorded. Long after you have forgotten the actual story, you will be preparing a talk that requires an illustration on how we allow circumstances to affect your attitude. For example, a quick search of the word *attitude* uncovers the "Pink Mommy" story and you have an illustration your audience will identify with.

NETWORK

The final resource of illustrations that we often pass up completely is the resource of network. Many popular men and women on the speaking circuit rely on a steady stream of articles, book excerpts, and observations passed on to them by friends and associates. You may not have the budget to hire someone to research illustrations for you, but you do have friends and associates. Use the Internet to solicit your followers and friends for personal stories.

About three years ago I started asking my friends to send me cartoons, illustrations, magazine articles, and quotes that struck them as unique and interesting. Those informal requests provide a constant source of great illustrations I would never have discovered on my own. My sister sent me the following quote: "Christianity is a lot like football. There are 22,000 people in the stands who desperately need exercise watching 22 people on the field who desperately need rest." I have used this over and over to illustrate life in general. Most people are spectators. We need more warriors.

A mental note is no note at all.

I also subscribe to several Internet sources that provide humor and stories I would never find by reading one book at a time, and I highly recommend you do the same.

One last suggestion. In high school I worked hard to expand my vocabulary beyond the words *far out* and *cool*. Which should give you a pretty good idea of the prehistoric era during which I attended high school.

My English teacher encouraged us to learn a new word every day and use it in conversation the same day we learned it. The best way to remember names is to use the name immediately after hearing it. The same is true of a new illustration. Do more than just write it down. Use it in a sentence as you talk to people. Doing so will help you remember it and prepare you to use it with power when you deliver it in your speech.

RECORD

I have thousands of illustrations saved to my computer. But I have also lost count of the times I have seen or heard an excellent illustration and made a mental note of it without making a physical or digital note of it. A mental note is no note at all. Someone can share a joke that makes me roar with laughter, I make a mental note to share it with my family, and then I forget the whole joke within seconds. All I remember is that I made a note of some kind. I have no idea what the story was or why I wanted to make a note of it. If you take away only one piece of advice from this chapter, grab on to this: A mental note is no note at all.

When you hear, see, or read a good illustration, write it down! Record it! Put it in your iPhone! Text yourself! Anything, but never trust your memory.

Einstein said that he never wasted brain power trying to remember what could be written down. Most of us don't have that much brain power to waste. An old Chinese proverb says, "The faintest ink has a better memory than the sharpest brain." When you observe something that has the potential of a good illustration, your hand should go to your pocket faster than lightning.

Record the details of the illustration and, the instant you are aware of it, how you think it could be used. This also applies to those rare original thoughts that come to you at unexpected times. Often when listening to other speakers, I find their words will trigger a tangential thought in my mind. Rather than try to juggle that thought and listen to the speaker at the same time, I record it immediately for later development.

Some of the best ideas come to me just before I go to sleep. You should always keep some means of recording your thoughts right by your bed. Believe it or not, a pad and pencil work best for this. I used to keep a small recorder by my bed until one night in the dark I dictated a wonderful illustration into the remote control for the television. One night I awoke from a dream that left me in a cold sweat. I knew the dream would make an excellent illustration, so I reached for my pad and pencil. In the dark I wrote my most prominent memory of the dream and fell back to sleep. As soon as I awoke I quickly reached for the pad. Scrawled across the center of the pad was the word "chicken." To this day I have no idea what the dream was about or what a chicken had to do with it.

Whether you are lying in bed or wide awake sitting in a dentist chair, record the illustration or idea in detail or you will forget it.

Look. Read. Journal. Network. Record. If you follow these steps consistently, you will have more illustrations than you can use. To get the most out of this pool of resources, it is important to have some way of filing and retrieving them when you need them. Thank God for the

Internet. Here are some suggestions on how you can use this amazing tool to file each kind of illustration.

With the very first illustration you record, determine what topic or topics that illustration speaks to and create folders with those names. File the illustration in detail in those folders.

....

An old Chinese proverb says, "The faintest ink has a
better memory than the sharpest brain."

....

There is no need to build a huge file overnight. Create the folders as you go. If you see an illustration today that would work well in a talk on leadership, create that folder. You will soon find yourself copying and pasting into a large database of illustration folders that will prove invaluable.

Of course, you might forget the topic someday. Thanks to computers, if you remember a word or sentence from the illustration, a simple word search of your illustrations file will find it.

Do not give in to the temptation to keep illustrations written on napkins and other scrapes of paper. I can speak from experience in saying you will never be able to find them when you need them. This may be a great solution in an emergency, but always transfer your observations to digital form and file them as soon as possible.

A special process for recording illustrations from books

The process for recording illustrations found in books follows a slightly different progression that will allow you to keep the best illustrations of the book without destroying the enjoyment of your reading. I owe my thanks to my friend Jim Green for this system.

1. Read with your illustration radar fine-tuned.
2. As you read put a pencil check in the margin beside passages that strike you as significant.
3. When you have finished reading for that day, record the page numbers of all your check marks on the inside of the back cover

of the book along with any topic you would assign to that passage. You need to record the page number only once, even if there is more than one passage checked on that page.

4. After you have finished the book, review all checked passages. Some of the passages will no longer seem relevant because they are not being read in the context of the book. Those will not be relevant to the listener either. If the passage can stand alone as an illustration, leave the check; if not, erase it.

5. At this point you have the option of entering each of these passages into your illustration file along with the name of the book, author, page number, date of publication, and city and name of the publisher. Or you can simply enter the name of the topic, a brief explanation of the illustration, the name of the book, and the page number. In that case you go to the book to retrieve the illustration. This is what I do. The only disadvantage of this option is you cannot access the illustration if you are not in the same location as the book. I may be one of the few people who still enjoy reading a book with actual pages and margins to write in. If you read from a digital source, this process is greatly simplified.

It takes a lot of time to find and file illustrations correctly, but the effort will be rewarded many times over by the freshness and power evident in your speeches.

PART II

THE PRESENTATION: THE SCORRE DELIVERY

Involving the Audience

You Are Always on My Mind

Chapter 6 dealt with the three elements of the total communication picture. Although SCORRE is the heart of your presentation, adding an effective opening and closing completes a powerful package that's likely to impact your audience long after you finish talking.

That's the goal: changed lives.

But an excellent presentation must reach beyond the paper to involve the audience, even in the preparation process. After all, it really is about them—your audience. And the audience is what this chapter is all about.

I used to be enthralled with the old philosophical riddle that asked, "If a tree falls in the forest and no one hears it, does it make a sound?" Some would argue that sound becomes sound only when the sound waves actually hit the ear and is perceived as sound. Until it is actually heard, it is only potential sound.

The same argument can be applied to communication. If a speaker speaks and there is no one there to listen (or if no one chooses to listen), communication does not take place. Some have gone so far as to say that communication does not take place until the listener is moved to action. I tend to agree. The audience is an essential part of the communication equation.

Often we are so concerned with speaking well that we forget the other half of the communication team, the audience. Without them there can be no communication. To be successful, the speaker must touch his audience. The more they are involved in the communication process, the more attentive they will be and the longer they will retain what they hear. The audience must be considered even way back in the very first step in preparing a speech: choosing a subject.

According to an article in *Bottom Line* magazine, "The human brain gets 87 percent of its information from the eyes and only 9 percent from the ears."[1] Pedagogues in England suggest that we remember 10 percent of what we hear, 30 percent of what we see, 60 percent of what we see and hear, and 80 percent of what we see, hear, and do.

Although the least effective method of communication is straight lecture, we often use only that one method. However, we are not limited to just flapping our gums. From the beginning of time, speakers and teachers have augmented lecture with object lessons, visual aids, and physical demonstrations of what they taught.

The Bible contains many stories of Jesus speaking to his loyal followers. In most cases, he used ordinary objects and events to illustrate key points. A mustard seed to illustrate the power of faith. A woman's lost coin to illustrate the value of each of God's children. Changing water into wine and asking the disciples to cast their fishing nets on the opposite side of the boat were not parlor tricks to entertain the crowds; they were illustrations of the truths he was teaching. They captured his followers' attention and solidified in their minds that experience and the truth attached to it.

In this chapter I will give you ideas on how you can bring your talk from the level of a lone tree falling in the woods to its fullest potential as a roaring wave of life-changing truth in the ears of your listeners.

INVOLVE YOUR AUDIENCE IN YOUR PLANNING

As you prepare your speech, the audience should never be far from your mind. After all, the objective you have worked so hard to develop has meaning only as it relates to the audience.

Sales managers, coaches, teachers, and preachers speak to virtually the same people every week. Yet each week that same group of people make up a different audience. One time they'll be festive and jubilant, and the next they'll be introspective and quiet. Those changes can happen even between morning and evening of the same day. In fact, if you deliver a boring talk, their mood may change even while you speak.

If you speak to the same people week after week, try, as you prepare, to anticipate what they will be like this week. What current events or corporate drama is affecting their mood and attitude? Keep your audience in mind throughout the entire preparation process.

When you are invited to speak to outside organizations, find out what age the audience will be and what kind of programming will precede your presentation. Ask your host to give you some insight into the personality of the people you will be addressing and the challenges they are facing. Are they reserved, intellectual, fun loving?

Occasionally an audience's attitude will change during a meeting. If that happens you may not necessarily want to change your entire speech, but you had better be prepared to adjust how you deliver your presentation accordingly.

I often speak for charitable organizations. During one recent speaking engagement, just before I took the platform a young woman whose life had been impacted by the work of this charity, told her heart-wrenching story. I had planned to begin my talk with a hilarious illustration designed to win the audience over, but considering the present mood of the audience, that no longer seemed appropriate. They had already been won over not by humor but in a more somber way. I opened with remarks that acknowledged the testimonial of the previous speaker and tied the first part of my message to what she said.

Later in the talk I was able to introduce humor to great advantage in my appeal for the audience to support the charity.

One of the best ways to engage an audience is to be fully present. Never show up just before you talk. Arrive early to watch what happens before you take the stage. Watch how the audience responds to what is going on.

Keep your audience in mind from the beginning of preparation all the way through the delivery. They are the focus of your communication.

INVOLVE YOUR AUDIENCE IN THINKING

Involving your audience in thinking is not the same thing as making them guess what in the world you are trying to say. An unfocused presentation will make them think all right. But not about your talk. Minds will soon begin to wander and think about the tasks that need to be done at home or the business deal that needs to be closed.

Over the years students have asked if providing the audience with an outline of the presentation was helpful. Simple outlines of the heart of your talk help hold interest because they tend to make your audience anticipate the development of that outline and more importantly give them a tool to remember the essence of the talk.

You can make the outline from a presentable form of your objective sentence and the rationale to support it. Leave room between elements of your rationale for the audience to take notes on the details of your delivery.

Here's how that could work. Let's suppose your objective sentence reads:

- Every person can experience life fully alive by living out three principles.

The corresponding outline might look like the one below. Remember to keep it simple. You don't need to put the entire talk in the outline.
Principles that lead to living fully alive

- Live with nothing to _____
- Live with nothing to _____
- Live with nothing to _____

Notice that this outline raises more questions than it answers. That's good. The function of your presentation is to answer the questions. The outline gives a structure for the listener to take notes and be reminded of where you are going and where you are on the journey.

Near the beginning of this presentation I might make a statement like: "How many of you want to live? No, I mean how many of you want to really live fully alive and have a ton of fun along the way?" (Audience responds.) "Good! At sixty-five I found the path to that kind of life and look forward to showing you some principles that can take you there."

Get the audience thinking along the same lines as your subject. Asking a question engages them in the process and prepares them for what is to come. This kind of opening makes the listener look forward with anticipation to hear what those steps might be.

INVOLVE YOUR AUDIENCE IN WRITING

I think one of the greatest compliments a speaker can receive is to see the audience taking notes. I want them to record their own tangled thoughts so they can give full attention to the rest of my message. So I encourage note-taking and often provide an outline like the one above for them to do so. A note of caution. Keep "fill in blanks" to a minimum. Anything that distracts from your presentation should be eliminated. Tell your audience that you will provide complete notes at the end of your presentation. That frees them to listen to you.

INVOLVE YOUR AUDIENCE IN ACTION

Nothing will imprint the truth of your message more firmly in the hearts of your audience than if you give them the opportunity to act on what they have heard. At times that will be done individually; other times in small groups.

It is popular now to have an audience break into small groups to discuss aspects of the presentation. This is a great learning tool as long as it doesn't break an important flow in your talk. I like to build momentum during my presentations and sometimes find it difficult to restart momentum that has been slowed by this technique. Having said that, there can be time left at the end of a presentation for application and a small group discussion of how what you are teaching can be applied in real life.

*Nothing will imprint the truth of your message more
firmly in the hearts of your audience than if you give them
the opportunity to act on what they have heard.*

If you involve your audience, it will move you into a new realm of communication. Instead of your talks being performances, they become experiences. The audience becomes a part of your presentation. This requires careful, creative preparation, and constant caution not to let the technique diffuse the focus of the message. In the long run, increased interest, retention, and understanding can make it worth the effort.

Using Effective Body Language

Let Your Body Talk

Appearances can be deceiving. How many times have you judged some-one on the basis of outward appearance only to discover you were wrong? A sloppily dressed person may surprise you with the delivery of a well-organized, persuasive speech. But first you must overcome the barrier of that first impression. Likewise the importance of a well-prepared speech may be lost if the communicator delivers that speech without passion or expression. Body language, voice inflection, facial expression, and gestures convey the conviction that makes you believable. This chapter deals with how you can use your body to enhance the power of your communication.

VOICE

Most speakers are not loud enough, even with a microphone. A micro-phone does not improve vocal strength or articulation. It only makes you louder.

In order for your audience to connect with your message, they first have to hear you. Adjust your volume to make use of all three levels of vocal projection:

- **Minimal voice** is the smallest volume that can be heard in a particular venue.
- **Maximal voice** is the loudest volume that can be tolerated in a particular venue.

- **Optimal voice** is the volume used throughout any presentation to deliver the majority of your talk. It is your natural voice and is comfortable to speak and easy on the listener.

Minimal and maximal voices are used for emphasis or character. They are "places to go" vocally to accentuate or stress a point or establish a different character in your narrative. It can also be used strategically to reengage a drifting audience, to draw them in and prepare them for a key point in your presentation.

To vocally prepare for a presentation, you can try a variety of warm-up techniques. Singing in full voice is an excellent vocal warm-up, even if you're not a singer. Memorize a few handy tongue twisters to jump-start teeth, tongue, lips, and brain. Practicing your presentation out loud ahead of time will help you identify built-in tongue twisters in your talk that can be remedied ahead of time. What is clever and interesting to read may not be so easy to speak. Also, over-articulation (during both practice and delivery) assures a clear, understandable presentation.

BE AWARE OF YOUR APPEARANCE

Some of you cringed when you read that. Why should communicators be concerned about how they look? Isn't that shallow? No. Whether we like it or not, the audience we are trying to reach is impacted by outward appearance. Sloppy dress, outdated styles, and poor choice of clothing can distract and cause the audience to prejudge the value of what you are about to say. As much as I try to concentrate on the content of the speech, I even find myself distracted by careless dressing. Anything that distracts the audience from the accomplishment of the objective is a liability. It isn't about vanity; it's about excellence.

Here are some principles that may keep you from hindering your communication efforts.

1. BE STYLISH, BUT DON'T OVERDO IT.

It is always a good rule to dress slightly more formally than the audience. This doesn't mean the speaker has to wear a designer suit or dress;

it simply means that your appearance should convey the idea that you are to be taken seriously. You should strive to be stylish enough not to distract by being old-fashioned, and conservative enough not to distract by being flamboyant. As a communicator you are trying to make a statement, but usually not a fashion statement.

Your audience should determine how you will dress. When speaking to the corporate executives of IBM, dress accordingly. When speaking to youth, be careful not to be too formal, but dress your age. I worked with youth for many years and became fully aware of their obsession with style and dress. I'm sure they would be distracted if at camp I got up to speak in a three-piece business suit.

As a teenager, however, I was always distracted by the other extreme: the forty-year-old speaker who dressed like a teenager. The knees of anyone over thirty are not usually a pretty sight. Teenagers don't expect adults to dress exactly like them to be accepted, but they will expect you to be up-to-date.

Not only is it important to wear the appropriate clothing, but it is also important to know how to wear it. I am always distracted watching a man try to communicate a serious and intelligent message with a tie that reaches only halfway to his belt. This is especially bad if the skinny part of the tie is hanging two inches below the wide part. Most people would have a difficult time taking such a person seriously.

I used to laugh at the concept of color coordination until I was made to realize that we live in a society that is very aware of poor color combinations. On more than one occasion I have been thankful to have a wife who sent me back to the closet to take off the orange tie because it didn't go with the navy suit.

Here are some simple rules:

- When traveling, bring clothes that will give you flexibility. Nothing is more uncomfortable than arriving at an informal gathering in formal clothes or vice versa.
- When in doubt lean toward the conservative.
- Ask your host what is appropriate. Don't be afraid to require clarification. Business casual can mean anything from tennis shoes, jeans, and a shirt, to a suit without a tie.

2. KEEP CLEAN AND WELL GROOMED.

Years ago I received a video tape of a speech I had given in front of eleven thousand people. I heard my children chuckling as they watched the tape. I was mortified to see that I had given that entire speech with several hairs on the back of my head sticking straight up in the air. Not only did it show up on the small television we were watching, but at the actual event my image had been projected larger than life on a thirty-foot screen. Those few hairs must have looked like palm trees swaying in the breeze. No one walked out of the meeting because of those hairs, but I am sure that they were a distraction. Well-kept hair, freshly ironed clothes, clean fingernails, shined shoes, and fresh breath are all an important part of a professional appearance.

3. DO A LAST-MINUTE CHECK.

Few speakers approach the microphone intending to look disheveled and unkempt, but unless you do a last-minute check you could easily give an impassioned speech with one side of your collar sticking straight up. On three separate occasions I have tried to communicate to an audience who could not listen because I had neglected to check my fly. Trust me, you cannot upstage an open fly.

I watched in amazement one night as a woman gave an entire speech with an earring caught in her hair. Through the entire speech, it hung just below her jaw, suspended by an invisible thread of hair. It seemed to be floating there magically. What did she talk about? I have no idea.

Before you move to the front of any room to do any kind of communication, make a last-minute check of your hair, tie, buttons, zippers, shirt tail, and accessories.

MAKE USE OF EFFECTIVE EYE CONTACT

"Look at me when I'm speaking to you." How many times has a parent used those words to establish eye contact with a child? The most well-prepared speech delivered with poor eye contact will lose much of its effectiveness. The eyes convey sincerity and conviction.

All the passion you can muster in the tone of your voice as you proclaim, "I love you," will not register if you don't look into the eyes of the one you say you love. Few people will buy a used car from a salesperson with shifty eyes. If a person won't look at you, you feel she can't be trusted. Lack of good eye contact will be interpreted by your audience as a lack of confidence, insincerity, apathy, or outright deception. Recognize and avoid the bad habits associated with poor eye contact.

DON'T BE A SWEEPER

One of the most common bad habits among speakers is the practice of sweeping the audience without ever focusing on any one person. An audience is simply a group of individuals. If you neglect to recognize those individuals by never establishing personal eye contact, your whole audience will feel left out. Even though you may not look at every person, your presentation will be much more personal if you establish eye contact with individuals. Don't be a sweeper. Look into the eyes of people in your audience.

DON'T BE A SHIFTER

A shifter can establish individual eye contact, but only for a brief moment. As soon as eye contact is made, this person quickly shifts the contact to another person. This looks like fear or shame or dishonesty, anything but confidence. This undesirable habit will cause your audience to think that you are ashamed or have something to hide. Shifty eyes have always been associated with someone who can't be trusted. Don't be a shifter.

DON'T BE A BIRD WATCHER

The speaker with the bird-watcher habit occasionally acknowledges the audience with a glance or two but spends much of the time focusing on random objects in the room. While talking the bird watcher gazes out the window, examines flaws in the molding, or finds any other safe haven that will keep him or her from seeing real people. I once watched a man give an entire message watching a spider crawl across the ceiling. Instead of being focused on the speaker, most of the eyes in the room were on the spider. I had a professor who would examine her nails as she lectured.

Nothing other than people in your audience should capture your attention. Professional stage entertainers are taught early in their careers not to be distracted by backstage sound or movement. They are taught to avoid looking at the bird that has somehow found its way into the theater. Don't be a bird watcher.

DON'T BE A DREAMER

The dreamer is the speaker who gazes into empty space during the entire presentation. This presenter seems to be in a trance. They give the impression that a bird could land on the podium and they wouldn't see it. Unfortunately, the audience listening to a dreamer will often conclude that there is also nothing between this speaker's ears. The most intelligent presentation delivered by a speaker who seems to be in another world will not be received with the respect it deserves.

DON'T BE A READER

The reader finds sanctuary from personal eye contact by keeping his head buried in a script. Although a motivated audience might survive such a delivery, most audiences will quickly lose interest. Even if you prepare scripted talks, it is important to be familiar enough with that message to be able to look up and acknowledge your audience. Speeches involving technical information are often scripted. Even in these talks, when you come to an illustration or clarification that does not require reading, look up! Tell the story! Ask the question. Then go back to your script. If you intend to read a speech, it would save a lot of time and effort simply to hand out printed copies and let the audience read it. Don't be a reader. Establish the habits of good eye contact.

═

Now that I've acknowledged the don'ts of eye contact, here are a few dos to keep you on the right track:

SPEAK TO INDIVIDUALS

An audience is made up of individuals who want to be acknowledged. One evening I watched a speaker get up and spend about thirty seconds looking around the audience, making eye contact with many of the people there. Occasionally he would nod or smile as someone acknowledged the eye contact. Just as I began to wonder if he was ever going to speak, the man took a deep breath and said, "I can see that I am going to enjoy the next half hour." Wow, what a way to win over an audience. Basically he was saying, "I see you and I like you." Even those who had not been directly affected by his kind gaze felt that he was aware of their presence.

As you speak, pick out individuals in the audience and speak directly to them. Make sure you include those who sit farther back and at the edges of your audience.

COMPLETE A THOUGHT WITH ONE PERSON

In a society that craves intimacy and fears it at the same time, eye contact can be a little uncomfortable. I tell my students that they should "look until it hurts." In other words, they should hold the eye contact with a single individual until it begins to feel uncomfortable. Finish a thought, stay with the person for several sentences. It can seem like an eternity, but the practice of good eye contact makes a very positive connection with the audience. Most people want to be acknowledged. Look at people. Let them know that you know they are there.

I am always asked if eye contact will make the audience uncomfortable and turn them off. I can't remember ever seeing someone establish such intense eye contact that it negatively affected communication, but I have seen hundreds unwittingly communicate a lack of confidence and even shame by their refusal to acknowledge the individuals in the audience with sustained eye contact.

KNOW HOW TO HANDLE LARGE AUDIENCES

In a large audience it is still important to practice the principles of good eye contact. Even when you cannot make out the faces of those in the back of the auditorium, pick out one person and complete a thought with that person. Imagine that it is just the two of you in a conversation, and communicate your thought with sincerity and personal conviction. If you speak to no one, no one will think you are speaking to him or her.

On the other hand, it has been proven that if you pick out someone far back in the audience and speak directly to that person, many seated near that person will believe you are speaking to them.

Many times I find myself speaking in situations where I can see absolutely nothing. The auditorium lights have been dimmed and two or three spotlights render me legally blind. I used to struggle in these situations until a wise friend who was actually close to legally blind shared a secret. "I can't see a thing beyond my notes," he confided. "So I direct my comments to specific friends I know. I may not be looking at Mr. Smith, but I visualize this friend in my mind's eye and talk to him personally. Then I talk to little Jenny Horton for a while. In this way my audience is never aware that I can't see who they are."

This man in his seventies is one of the finest communicators I have ever met. Even though he can't see, he talks to individual people.

PRACTICE UNTIL GOOD EYE CONTACT IS NATURAL

Developing the habit of good eye contact does not come easily. It takes a lot of practice. Have friends or your spouse constantly critique your eye contact. Describe a dreamer, shifter, and sweeper and ask them to point out when you slip into those bad habits. My wife reminds me when I slip into the habit of speaking to only one side of the room. I have excellent eye contact; it's just that I tend to discriminate and give it to only half the audience. I have no idea why I do this, but I treat the audience on the right side of the room as though they don't exist, and it is only with her help that I became aware of it and have worked hard to correct it.

You can also practice with a video camera. Place the camera somewhere in the audience, and as you speak make a conscious effort to use good eye contact. Include the camera. That's right! Pretend the camera is a person and make several attempts to look into the lens and complete a thought. When you watch this video you will immediately spot any tendency to shift or sweep, and you will be amazed at the power of eye contact when your own gaze comes to rest on you. You might even get motivated by your own talk. Video is a powerful tool for growing in excellence as a communicator. Use it often to check up on your eye contact.

Daily conversation provides another opportunity for practice. Look at people as you converse with them. Don't just look in their direction or stare through them; look into their eyes. Then practice the same kind of eye contact with large groups.

CREATE FACIAL EXPRESSIONS TO MATCH YOUR WORDS

Have you ever watched a speaker deliver a motivational message with an expression that seemed more appropriate for attending the funeral of a favorite pet?

When someone says, "Boy, was that speaker enthusiastic!" he is not describing the words but the facial expressions, the body language, and the tone of voice that accompanied the words.

Your face makes the audience believe that you believe what you say. When you really believe what you say, your whole body gets involved. Can you picture a woman walking slowly down the corridor of her apartment building repeating quietly, in a monotone voice, "Fire. Fire. Help. The building is on fire"? Of course not. If such a scene should occur, I doubt anyone would pay attention. But such a scene would never happen. A woman with that kind of urgent message would be wide-eyed, waving her arms, and screaming at the top of her lungs, "Fire! Fire!"

When you speak of joy, does your face show it? I constantly remind my friends in ministry that you cannot communicate the joy of faith, with a face that looks as though you have just swallowed a profusely sweating toad. Can people see in your body language those things that make you sad? Does your expression leave no doubt that you are excited about what you proclaim?

....

Your face makes the audience believe that you believe what you say.
When you really believe what you say, your whole body gets involved.

....

One student responded to that challenge by saying, "Oh, I can do that. I took drama classes for three years in college." He missed the point.

There is no need to act. Simply allow your whole body to communicate. Of all people, communicators ought to be the ones who wear their hearts on their sleeves and who let it show on their faces.

Of course, it is possible to get too emotional and hinder your communication, but in all my years of teaching I have seen only a few who carry body language to the extreme. Most don't even begin to tap the potential of this aspect of communication.

Before you give your next presentation, deliver it into a mirror or digital camera. Ask yourself, "If I were listening to this person, would I think that he or she was excited about what is being said? Would the enthusiasm make me want to hear more?" Ask, "How would I express myself if I were sharing this with a close friend?" If messages were delivered with half the excitement we use in everyday conversation, audience interest would pick up dramatically.

USE EFFECTIVE GESTURES

The same advice given above applies to gestures. We walk around all day waving our arms and making extensive use of our hands as we communicate to everyone around us. But when we step up to speak it's as though the arms are hollow and someone has poured them full of cement. Or in front of an audience we repeat one gesture over and over like a robot with a short circuit. Nervous tension and habit are the culprits. Relax and carry your gestures to their fullest extent.

FLIPPERS

Tension turns even experienced speakers into flippers. Flippers let their arms hang like lead at their sides, and all their gestures are reduced to a little helpless flipping motion of the hands. It doesn't matter whether the speaker is describing a tiny breath of wind or a major hurricane; the same anemic flip of the wrist is used to describe both.

PRISONERS

I have watched speakers interlock their fingers at about waist level and then deliver a speech with movement that looked like an anemic effort to get them unlocked. Occasionally the thumbs will point upward or a finger will move in a desperate effort to be free, but the hands stay locked.

POCKET LOVERS

Unless you want people to be guessing what is in your pockets, it is a good idea to keep your hands out of them. Although a hand in the pocket may seem like a casual and relaxed gesture, it is really no gesture at all. If you don't move the hand in your pocket, you will look stiff and uncomfortable. If you move your hand, the audience will begin taking odds on what you are fumbling with. Free yourself up! Let your hands paint the pictures your lips describe.

FLAPPERS

Occasionally I run across a flapper (one whose gestures are so exaggerated that they detract from the message), but it is extremely rare. More common is repetitive, meaningless gestures that annoy beyond description. Car salesmen on television are experts at this. The best way to see if you have this habit is to record a performance and play it back in fast forward. After you stop weeping with laughter, you will resolve to stop repetitive gestures.

My friend McNair Wilson has identified many other abhorrent and distracting gestures, like "digital dating" (fingertips playfully fidgeting with one another as you talk) or "spider doing pushups on a mirror" (fingertips moving inward and outward, over and over again). The point is this: There is no such thing as a neutral gesture. Everything you do with your hands communicates something. Make sure your hands are not giving a speech in competition with the one you are delivering.

It was only after repeated suggestions from my wife that I took the time to watch a video presentation to see one of these gremlins in my own presentation. Out of habit I would constantly pinch my nose. In one speech alone I reached up and grabbed my nose twenty-one times. Evidently this was a comforting confirmation that there was nothing on my nose, but it did nothing to enhance my talk and I was totally unaware that I was doing it.

At an Easter service I heard one of the finest messages on the resurrection ever presented. Unfortunately the pastor had a distracting habit that no one had ever been kind enough to bring to his attention. As he began a dramatic phrase he would pull his head down until it looked as though he had no neck. Then as he delivered the phrase he would increase in volume and slowly, with a jerky mechanical kind of motion, extend his neck to its maximum length. After the service we were invited to attend a luncheon along with other visitors to the church. The conversation in several groups centered not around the excellent content of the pastor's message, but the unique turtle-like quality of the pastor's neck.

Saturday Night Live creates many of its sketches off the quirks and gestures of presidents and popular figures. They look for the annoying idiosyncrasies and exaggerate it for the sake of a laugh. However, it isn't so funny if it is you the audience is laughing at after a professional presentation.

Practice with the mirror, record your presentations, and seek constructive critique from friends. These are errors of nervous energy that we rarely commit in casual conversation. If you think of your speech as a conversation with a friend, it will help you relax. The only difference between talking with a friend and talking to a group is the number of friends in the room.

Very seldom will you find someone in your audience willing to risk telling you that you look like a turtle. So it is of utmost importance that you use video and the constructive critique of friends to help you spot those distracting motions and exorcise them from your presentations.

STAND AND DELIVER

One very important aspect of your communication is the way you stand. I have watched communicators of every age, sex, and ability sway rhythmically as they speak, causing seasickness in a significant proportion of the audience.

I have watched as they paced like a caged lion or simply walked in small circles like a bewildered animal. I've seen speakers draped on the podium like a tiger in the afternoon sun, or watched as a person shifted weight from one foot to another with a frequency that caused me to worry if the hip joint would hold. I have been guilty of rooting myself on one side of the platform to deliver the entire speech to one side of the audience. Most of these tendencies can be corrected by practicing correct posture and stance.

To communicate with authority and confidence, stand with your feet slightly apart and one foot slightly ahead of the other. With your weight evenly distributed between both feet, bend slightly at the waist and lean toward the audience. Communicate a complete thought. When you move, move with purpose. Emphasize your next point with a different segment of the audience. Random pacing is very distracting. Get where you want to be, take a solid stand, and communicate again.

Stand on your own two feet. Avoid leaning against podiums, music stands, or other people on the platform. You may laugh, but I consider any solid object on the stage—mike stand, podium, stool—as a person. You would not lean on, fondle with, or drape yourself across a person standing on the stage, so try not to molest the other items that might be there.

In conclusion, the object is not to become an actor or entertainer who plays with people's emotions, but to allow your body to express the concepts and emotions you are presenting with your lips.

Let your body talk.

Maximizing the Communication Environment

Killing the Gremlins

One evening while listening to a speaker I found myself strangely depressed. The speaker was excellent, the message well prepared and to the point, yet I couldn't shake this dreary feeling. About halfway through the presentation I realized what was causing it.

I couldn't see anything. The lighting was perfect for candlelight dining or sleeping in an overstuffed chair but completely incompatible for any kind of presentation. The only lights bright enough to light the platform were straight overhead and threw foreboding shadows over the eyes of anyone who ventured near the podium. To make matters worse, the sound system gave the speaker's voice a tinny quality and rang with an annoying squeal whenever his voice hit a certain tone.

On top of all this, at those moments when the speaker dared to raise his voice to emphasize a point, the person running the sound system, in a vain attempt to save the already shattered speakers, completely muted his voice.

It was painful to listen to the presentation, especially knowing that I would be speaking from the same platform later in the day. I quietly slipped from the room and sought out the audio-visual staff. Audio-visual was actually an oxymoron in this situation. The hotel ballroom where this happened had neither good sound nor good light. Silent darkness would have better described the situation. I vowed never to be caught in this situation again.

Let's look at the steps you can take to control your environment and enhance the effectiveness of your communication.

LET THERE BE LIGHT

Lighting sets the atmosphere of a room. The atmosphere in that hotel ballroom was rendered impersonal and boring by the faceless bodies that stumbled to and from the podium. Furthermore, the faces were made downright spooky by the angle of the inadequate lighting coming from above.

Effective communication is only possible when the communicator's face is visible. When the communicator's eyes are visible, the effectiveness is increased another hundredfold.

Many people have become so accustomed to poor lighting that they are not consciously aware of its negative effect. But it does have an effect.

I was once asked to speak at a gathering of about eight hundred people. When I arrived I discovered that the lighting was terrible. The venue was a huge gymnasium, and the only light came from dim incandescent bulbs high in the ceiling. How they played basketball in this place I will never know.

Before the program started I watched as one of the organizers of the event walked across the totally unlit stage located at one end of the gymnasium. Even from where I was in the third row, I could not see any of the features on his face. I couldn't tell whether he was smiling or frowning or whether he had been born without a face. I can't imagine that the people in the back even knew he was there.

I make maximum use of facial expression in my presentations, yet I was being asked to communicate in almost total darkness. I begged the sponsor to find some way to light that stage. I had kindly requested adequate lighting months before, but those requests had been ignored. The argument was that because they had never used additional lighting in the past, they saw no reason to start now. I could tell that my host was angry about my insistence on throwing some light on the stage, but I was persistent.

After some scrambling he located a bright halogen light used for a home movie camera and improvised a stand to hold it. It was far from perfect, but the harsh light provided enough illumination so everyone could see my face.

For the first fifteen minutes of the presentation, the audience responded with enthusiasm and spirit. Then suddenly the light went out, leaving me in darkness. I continued my presentation, but the dynamic of the audience changed immediately. Their laughter seemed forced and died away as quickly as it began. I never have trouble controlling a group, but within minutes I could hear young people in the back begin to conduct their own conversations. Finally someone discovered the plug had been kicked from the outlet and plugged it back in.

The instant the light came back on, there was spontaneous applause from the audience. Their attention snapped back to the stage, and the group responded with the same delighted enthusiasm that they had exhibited at the beginning of the program.

The audience would never have been conscious of the lack of light had they not been able to see clearly in the first part of the program, but its absence would have affected their attitudes and responses throughout the entire program. The host apologized profusely after the program. Later he admitted, "I never realized the difference that good lighting makes." He knows now!

Does the place where you speak look like a place to celebrate life, or is it more like a morgue?

Here is a test you can conduct to see whether the lighting in any situation is optimum for good communication. Have someone stand where you usually stand when you speak, then walk to the back of the room or auditorium.

- Give yourself a C+ if you can see clearly all the facial features of the person up front.
- Give yourself a B+ if there are no shadows in the eye sockets or under the nose. Lighting that is too close to the front and coming from too high will create hideous shadows that make the eyes look hollow and sunken, and give the speaker the appearance of a talking skull.

- Give yourself an A+ if you can see a pinpoint of light reflected in the eyes of the person up front.

Occasionally you may get an objection to good lighting. "There will be a bright light in the speaker's eyes." Well, that's an A+. That's the point. At first good lighting will always be a little uncomfortable for the speaker.

That is the kind of lighting that is most conducive to good communication. That kind of lighting makes a room feel warm and brightens the spirit of everyone listening. If you take out a recent professional photograph of yourself or a friend, you will see that pinpoint of light in the eye. It is so important to bringing life to the photo, that if it does not appear in the original print the photographer will add it digitally.

They say that the eyes are the window to the soul. The eyes are the first place to see indications that your child is sick or lying. Sincerity and integrity that can be communicated only with the eyes will be lost on the audience if the speaker's eyes cannot be seen. I have given substantial

LIGHT SET TOO HIGH   RESULTING SHADOWS

LIGHT SET JUST RIGHT   RESULTING SPARKLE

space to this subject because of the important role this overlooked factor has on communication.

For small groups you won't need professional lighting, but make sure the room is bright and cheery. When the size of your audience nears one hundred, additional lighting will usually be beneficial. If the room is relatively small, this can be done inexpensively. Light these

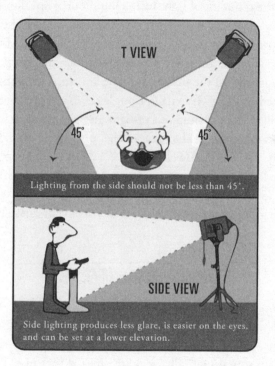

T VIEW

45°   45°

Lighting from the side should not be less than 45°.

SIDE VIEW

Side lighting produces less glare, is easier on the eyes, and can be set at a lower elevation.

rooms so that you can clearly see facial expressions and the pinpoint of light in the eye.

OBJECTIONS TO GOOD LIGHTING

Here is a simple review:

1. Facial expressions should be clearly visible from anywhere in the audience.

2. The lights should be positioned at a low enough angle to avoid casting shadows over the eyes. You can determine this by turning all the other lights off when you do the test. Lower the angle of the lights until the shadows are gone and stop at that point. Usually this is at forty-five degrees. The glare in the eyes of the speaker will be at a minimum.

3. Look for the pinpoint of light in the pupil of the speaker's eye. That pinpoint is a primary indication that the lights are bright enough and at a low enough angle. Remember that in larger auditoriums not everyone in the audience will be able to see that pinpoint, but those sitting toward the front should be able to. Two lights can be mounted at a forty-five-degree angle off to either side as long as they still create the pinpoint of light and are equal in intensity. Sometimes this reduces the glare in the speaker's eyes and allows the lights to be placed at a lower angle.

4. Make the light as unobtrusive as possible. Seldom do you want the platform to look like a night club stage. Use soft, defused light and flesh-tone gels to get the warm, well-lit effect that doesn't distract.

LET THOSE WHO WILL HEAR, HEAR

Know the importance of good quality sound.

Almost as bad and just as common as poor lighting is inadequate sound systems. Nothing distracts more than a poor quality reproduction and/or constant squealing feedback. I am amazed that in the twenty-first century you can still occasionally find this aberration at White House press briefings.

There are three reasons good sound reproduction is important for groups of more than one hundred. First, it enables everyone in the audience to hear clearly. Second, it saves strain on the speaker's voice. Third, it gives the speaker tremendous versatility in voice inflection. With a good sound system, even a whisper can be heard in the back of the room.

Know how to recognize good quality sound.

As with lighting, there are methods to determine whether you have or need a good quality sound system. Know that the need for a sound system is as dependent on the acoustics of a room as it is on the size. Some rooms resonate sound well enough so that you can talk in a normal voice and be heard easily by a hundred people. Other rooms soak up sound like a sponge and need a sound system for any significant sized group. Still other rooms reverberate sound, making anything the speaker says nearly unintelligible.

If you can speak softly and the entire audience can still hear what you say with ease, you probably don't need a sound system. If not, consider it mandatory.

If the system being used sounds tinny and thin, if it tends to give off feedback or a hollow-barrel kind of ringing when the speaker hits certain tones, you would do well to consider bringing in a system that helps rather than hinders your communication efforts. Hotel ballrooms are notorious for bad sound systems. Ask your host to provide a system that has adjustable equalization so that you can get rid of feedback in a variety of situations. Learn the names of quality systems and ask for them in your first communication with the host. Most importantly, arrive early and do a sound check before the program begins. Find the median volume and equalization that will accommodate all volume levels you will use in your presentation and then kindly ask the sound person to use that setting and not touch it during the program. Physical threats often help here.

KNOW HOW TO USE A MICROPHONE

1. If the microphone is attached to the podium, make sure it extends far enough back toward the speaker to be useful. Microphones work their best when they are within a few inches of your lips. There should be no need for you to do the entire presentation looking like the hunchback of Notre Dame.
2. During the sound check, hit the podium. Somehow podiums create scary booming noises and initiate feedback when bumped. Make sure your system is set to avoid it or that you are prepared to avoid touching the podium.

3. Ideally a microphone should be located at a forty-five-degree angle just below and almost touching your lips. If you position the microphone parallel to the floor and at lip height, you will get a popping sound every time you pronounce hard consonants like "p." Learn how to hold the mike.

4. When you remove a microphone from a stand, stop speaking and remove it carefully to avoid the noise that is generated by taking it from its holder. In the same vein, unless you want to create a sound like a garbage compacter, never adjust a gooseneck microphone holder without first removing the microphone.

5. Do not fondle the microphone or its stand. This distracting habit is common among singers and entertainers. It should never be the practice of an effective communicator.

6. Stay close to the microphone. This is a skill that I am still learning. Early in my career I got into the habit of holding the mike too far from my face. I still struggle to break that habit. Speakers who are not used to using a microphone often act as if it is electrified or filled with germs. It is filled with germs. Get used to it. You should never be more than a few inches from the microphone.

7. It is worth mentioning again that you should adjust the sound levels and height of the microphone before you begin speaking and then leave it alone. Chances are that you will remain the same height throughout the speech. Don't allow someone to keep adjusting the volume levels as you speak. These well-meaning people nullify the value of a microphone by trying to keep the volume the same level throughout the speech. You don't want the volume to be the same. One of the assets of the microphone is that it allows you to work with a wide variety of volumes. Don't let a sound engineer take that advantage from you. Make your requirements known to the sound technicians. Most of the time they will be happy to comply.

8. Finally, many speakers today use a headset microphone that eliminates many of the problems covered above. There are two basic problems with headset mikes. One is that ill-fitting ones will keep falling off your face. I have yet to find one that comfortably fits my enormous head. I have given serious thought to stapling them to my

head. The second problem is that the microphones in headsets tend to mute higher volumes and limit the ability to do sound effects. Take advantage of those early sound checks so you have time to make sure you are using the best mike for your presentation. If you are using a headset, make sure it fits or staple it in place.

When a microphone is used properly, the audience isn't even aware of it. Improperly used, it's a distraction that inhibits communication.

ONE SIZE DOESN'T FIT ALL

When you're trying to set up a good environment for communication, one of the most important rules to remember is to match the size of the room to the size of the audience. I would rather have 200 people crammed into a room that usually seats 150 than to have 1,000 people seated in the front rows of a 5,000-seat auditorium. Know ahead of time what your venue will look like and what size the audience will be. Always try to fill the room, even if that means changing the room.

Years ago I taught a class of teenagers in the auditorium of a large church. In an effort to maximize the use of space, another class was taught at the far end of the auditorium. Not only did we have to endure the sound distractions of having two groups in the same room, the constant hand signals being passed between the groups (no texting existed at the time) made communication in this environment an exercise in futility. Eventually we solved the problem by converting a room that had been used to store banquet tables to accommodate my class. The students helped me brighten the room with paint and additional lighting. They called the room "the happy dungeon," and their attention level and enjoyment of the sessions increased dramatically when we began to meet there.

Another time I taught a small class of adults that was moved from an auditorium to the living room of a nearby home. Again, the difference in the atmosphere affected the attitude of the group. There is nothing wrong with an auditorium, but there is something about a small group meeting in such a large place that makes the audience feel like a pea in a pail and sets a mood that is not conducive to good communication.

If you must speak to a small group in a large auditorium, have them seated together at the front. When people are all spread out, it communicates a coldness that affects their attitude and receptivity. Make as many of these arrangements as you can before you arrive and then go to the venue early to assess the situation. Once folks are seated you may need a bulldozer to get them to move.

LOOK OUT BEHIND YOU

Just as it is important to be seen if you are going to communicate, it is also important not to have other scenes creating a distraction as you speak. I have been in beautiful auditoriums that have glass fronts that display breathtaking scenery behind the speaker. The speaker should be the brightest image in front of the audience. If the background is bright, then the lighting must make the speaker even brighter.

I remember sitting in an audience where the speaker chose to stand in front of a large window that stretched from the ceiling to the floor. I spent the entire time trying to tear my attention from a cat that in plain view was ambushing a small clueless duck waddling through a flower garden. I wanted to listen but the slinking cat and potential demise of the clueless duck was much more fascinating.

In Alaska a speaker chose to stand with his back to a large picture window that looked out on a beautiful snow-covered landscape. Not only was the scenery distracting, but the brightness of the background rendered the speaker only a dark silhouette. I could hardly look toward the front because the brightness of the background hurt my eyes. It takes only a little planning to avoid these environmental hindrances to communication. The Alaskan speaker was wise. He quickly recognized that his audience was being blinded and moved to the other end of the room where the same light that had been so disruptive now illuminated rather than eliminated his face. It took less than two minutes to make the adjustment, and the effort saved the day.

More recently my friend and business partner Michael Hyatt spoke at a conference with his back to the windows of a high-rise. He was lighted appropriately, but as he began his talk window washers lowered their working platform into view behind him. Unexpected? Yes! Preventable? Probably not. Like a pro he delivered his message with passion, but he would be the first to admit it took tremendous concentration and effort to compete with a squeegee. Imagine if the window washers had brought a cat and a duck with them.

Here are some simple rules for watching what is behind you:

1. Don't ever stand in front of a window or bright lights to communicate. The back lighting will make your face only a shadow, it will be uncomfortable for the audience to look in your direction, and no matter how good you are you can't compete with scenery.
2. Avoid busy, brightly colored backgrounds. You should be the most interesting object in the front of the room.
3. Avoid standing in front of mirrors. Many hotel ballrooms have decorative mirrors surrounding the entire room. In this setting a spotlight or any light shining on you will be reflected right back into the audience's eyes. If you must speak in such a situation, hang a drape over the mirrors directly behind you.
4. Avoid having anything behind you that moves while you speak, especially cats and clueless ducks or children.
5. Eliminate intrusions into your communication environment. If you are the after-dinner speaker, ask catering to clear the plates before you speak. You can't compete with clattering china. In the best of circumstances communication is a difficult task. Make sure your environment is a help and not a hindrance.

Train yourself to be observant of the situations that have distracted you during other presentations and do everything in your power to eliminate those ahead of time. My team can walk into any venue and automatically spot what will hinder or help. Take the responsibility to create an environment to enhance your presentation. No one else will.

Having said that, if your hosts provide everything you need and some unavoidable glitch throws you a curve, do everything in your power to give your best presentation under the circumstance. When the going gets tough, professionals keep going. Your efforts will be well rewarded.

I once prepared to talk to an audience of two thousand in a breakout for a very large conference. My host was mortified when only about a dozen people materialized in this monstrous ballroom. The performer who went on before me panicked and bailed out three minutes into her act. I came down off the platform, had everybody pull chairs in a half circle, and gave them my best show. Because of the situation it was delivered in a much more intimate fashion, not as flashy and very interactive. My host was so grateful that he hired me for dozens of performances after that. Some of those shows were attended by more than ten thousand people. Because I had given him my best with twelve people, he honored me by putting me in front of thousands.

PART III

THE APPLICATION: THE SCORRE ADVANTAGE

Managing Your Time
Getting Out from Behind the Eight Ball

One day a bright young student raised his hand at the conclusion of the SCORRE Conference. "The material that I have learned here is invaluable," he said. "My problem is that I can't afford the time to prepare each of my talks with such meticulous care." Knowing that he had to prepare several talks each week, I understood his frustration. However, my response was not what he expected. I told him, "You can't afford not to take the time to prepare your talks with care."

I would extend the same challenge to you. Every speech, every lecture, every sermon deserves your best effort in preparation and delivery. If your message is not worth that effort, it's probably not worth presenting. If you are speaking so often that you don't have time to prepare your talks, you are speaking too often. It's all about managing your time.

That brings us to the skill of managing time. The biggest reason why people don't think they have the time to prepare adequately is that they have never learned to manage their preparation time. As a result they operate under an emergency system called crisis management. Crisis management is the approach you used back in high school when you waited until just before an assignment was due before beginning to work on it.

If you find yourself preparing Thursday night for a talk you are scheduled to deliver on Friday, you are operating under crisis management. If a preacher begins to prepare a sermon the same week it is to be delivered, that is crisis management. This kind of management undermines the potential of every talk you give. It robs them of clarifying illustrations and supportive research. Crisis management is the pathway to mediocrity.

---

*If you are speaking so often that you don't have time to
prepare your talks, you are speaking too often.*

Two simple lessons in time management can change that.

First, understand that the cost of saving time is time. In the long run the SCORRE system will save you time in preparation. However, you must be willing to invest the time up front to make it work.

If you speak on a weekly basis and want to be as excellent as possible, get away a couple of days each quarter to plan ahead.

Are you willing to take the time away from your everyday responsibilities to plan for excellence in the messages and speeches you will be giving in the coming months? The common response is, "I would love to do that, but I'm just too busy." Certainly my everyday needs would go unmet and your business would fall apart, right? Wrong!

The cost of saving time is time.

Look back on your life when sickness or emergency took you away from work for several days. When you returned, had your career crumbled or your business gone bankrupt? No! You probably picked up where you left off with hardly a blink. If sickness can take you from your work for two or three days without significant damage, imagine what three days of concentrated planning can do to enhance your speaking.

The wise money manager knows that if he wants to make money

over a period of time he must be willing to invest some money up front. You will never get beyond crisis management until you are willing to make an initial investment of time. If you are willing to commit to that investment, you can reap wonderful dividends in the quality of your communication.

Second, apply the principle of staying one speech ahead. A speech is like a good wine. The best are those that have had a chance to ferment and age. A good host would never serve a wine that had been in the bottle for only a week. Likewise there is no excuse for serving up a message that has not had time to ferment. If your preparation plan involves a little aging, new illustrations and ideas will present themselves as the speech ferments. You will find ways to clarify your objective that you never would have thought of without the benefit of time. You will be able to practice and evaluate. Time = excellence.

There are four stages in the development of any speech, sermon, or talk.

THE IDEA STAGE

The idea stage is where the speech is just a gleam in your eye. You have decided to address a subject but have not yet determined a specific focus for your talk or all that you want to talk about. At most you have a few ideas in mind and are beginning to list all the things you want to say and think about how you can make the speech dynamic.

THE SKELETON STAGE

During the skeleton stage of development you work your ideas through the SCORRE process. Write an objective sentence and develop your rationale. By the end of the skeleton stage, you've articulated exactly what the objective of your speech is and the rationale that will get you there.

THE OUTLINE STAGE

During the outline stage you add an opening and a closing and arrange your rationale and illustrations in outline form. You may even write out the speech in manuscript form. At the end of this stage of development, the speech is ready to deliver. But the excellent communicator would want the speech to go through one more process.

THE FERMENTATION STAGE

In the fermentation stage the finished speech is allowed to sit in the quiet cellars of your consciousness. Ideally every prepared speech should be given at least an additional week to interact with the enzymes of life. During this stage time becomes your best friend as you encounter events and observations that fit perfectly with your speech. You only notice them because they connect with the speech you worked so hard to prepare. You will not be making major changes during the fermentation process, but the additions and changes you do make will give your speech its final razor edge. At that point you are ready to serve up a vintage message.

—

The principle of staying one speech ahead requires that you work out a plan to begin working on speeches long before they are to be delivered and have them completed and fermenting at least one week ahead of time. The only way this will ever happen is if you make a commitment to get away and get a head start on the entire process.

If you have to deliver a new talk every week like many of my ministry friends, I recommend you set aside a couple of days each quarter dedicated exclusively to preparing three speeches in each of the stages mentioned above. Get three speeches in the outline stage and ready to ferment, three developed to the skeleton stage awaiting outline development, and three others in the idea stage. If you can do this in synergy with friends who are doing the same thing, the process will be even more valuable.

Start with the speech or speeches that need to be delivered first, and get them to the outline stage (ready to deliver). Next, work on the speeches that will be delivered at a later date and get them at least to the skeleton stage (objective sentence and rationale).

Finally, put together some of the ideas that you are going to be working on for later speeches. Include not only the subject and central theme but also notes on how you might develop the speech to meet the needs of your audience.

You will quickly discover that this is not a completely linear process. As you are working on the final touches of one speech, an idea for a brand-new one will pop into your brain. Write it down in your idea folder and then go back to working on your speech. Conversely, you may be working on the ideas for a new speech when the perfect illustration materializes for the speech you have to deliver next week.

This process is a godsend for those of us who are ADHD. It gives us four folders that can trap all those random thoughts that accost us.

The idea is that you never work on one speech from beginning to end in a single setting. Rather you move several speeches one step ahead each time you prepare. I can tell you from experience that this makes preparation a much more fun, creative process than the usual mode of scrambling to get tomorrow's speech done.

For example, you might put the final touches on the cost of leadership speech while the speech on overcoming sales objections continues to ferment. You could develop the outline for your talk on team building and begin fleshing out the embryo ideas for your speech on how to build raving fans (to be delivered in several weeks).

This way of working keeps you from always preparing at the last minute for the talk you are supposed to give in a few days. Even if you can't allow the finished product to ferment, it will have done so during the entire process of development. In the long run this kind of graduated planning and development not only will result in better speeches but in the end will save you time.

How to Use Humor in Communication

Funny—How That Works!

Victor Borge is accredited with saying, "Laughter is the shortest distance between two people." What a brilliant observation. Humor has opened thousands of doors for me to make presentations to hundreds of thousands of people around the world. It has been the foundation of a successful career that has spanned four decades. Most of all it has allowed me to make the kinds of presentations that have physically, mentally, and spiritually empowered the lives of millions of people. Humor comes naturally to me. I see the world in a different light. However, even if it does not come naturally to you, it is a skill that can be learned and developed.

Too many speakers avoid humor because so much of today's humor is degrading, angry, and hurtful. But it is my guess that if you make your living enriching lives in public speaking, this is not the kind of "humor" you are trying to develop.

The best definition of humor I have ever heard is this: "Humor is a gentle way to acknowledge human frailty." Put another way, humor is a way of saying, "I'm not okay and you're not okay, but that's okay." Humor is possible only when people are willing to acknowledge their imperfections. But a skillful communicator who can make an audience laugh (and is able to laugh at himself) opens the door to communicate life-changing information.

This chapter is designed to help you develop humor as a tool in your communication arsenal. It will show why humor is important, what makes something funny, and how you can use this valuable resource. It will help you determine what is appropriate, where to look for humor, and how you can practice this skill to fit your own communication style. Whether you think of yourself as a humorous person or not, whether you believe your audience will be receptive to humor or not, this chapter will give you the insights you need to develop this skill.

Humor is a way of saying, "I'm not okay and you're not okay, but that's okay."

THE VALUE OF HUMOR

Before you would even want to develop the skill of using humor in your communication, you would have to be convinced of its value. Humor is important for several reasons.

1. HUMOR BENEFITS THE MIND AND BODY.

Ice cream trucks used to prowl the streets of suburban neighborhoods selling their delicious varieties of heavenly taste. The driver was called the Good Humor Man. Why that title? The driver didn't tell jokes or wear a clown outfit. According to the Good Humor website, the driver got the name from the Good Humor brand of ice cream, which got its name from the Humor palate (where we carry our sense of taste). I doubt if that was the reason the public recognized him as the "good humor man." For them it was because of the reactions he elicited in the faces and hearts of hundreds of children when they heard the music played by the ice cream truck. Little eyes would sparkle and children would wake out of sound sleep to greet the man who drove that truck.

Audiences greet the speaker who effectively uses humor the same way. There is anticipation and excitement that causes the blood to flow and the mind to be more alert. Someone has said that humor is internal jogging. It's just plain good for you.

Humor is internal jogging. It's just plain good for you.

Years ago, journalist, author, and professor Norman Cousins chronicled the healing health benefits of laughter in his book *Anatomy of an Illness*. Cousins shared how he developed a debilitating arthritic illness that confined him to bed. The prognosis was not good. He asked to be removed from the depressing atmosphere of the hospital and was allowed to stay in a hotel where he could watch comedy movies and eat decent food. Here is what he said about his experience:

> It worked. I made the joyous discovery that ten minutes of genuine belly laughter had an anesthetic effect and would give me at least two hours of pain-free sleep. When the pain-killing effect of the laughter wore off, we would switch on the motion-picture projector again, and, not infrequently, it would lead to another pain-free sleep interval. Sometimes, the nurse read to me out of a trove of humor books. Especially usefully were E. B. and Katharine White's *Subtreasury of American Humor* and Max Eastman's *The Enjoyment of Laughter*.
>
> How scientific was it to believe that laughter—as well as the positive emotions in general—was affecting my body chemistry for the better? If laughter did in fact have a salutary effect on the body's chemistry, it seemed at least theoretically likely that it would enhance the system's ability to fight the inflammation. So we took sedimentation rate readings just before as well as several hours after the laughter episodes. Each time, there was a drop of at least five points. The drop by itself was not substantial, but it held and was cumulative. I was greatly elated by the discovery that there is a physiological basis for the ancient theory that laughter is good medicine.[1]

There have been times when I have struggled over whether or not to use humor in my presentations. Many times my talks contain serious material. Occasionally I am invited to preach in the Sunday morning service of a church. I ask myself, "In this situation is there any benefit to making people laugh?" The answer is a resounding yes!

I remember the first time a church asked me to come for the sole purpose of making the people laugh. That evening, I spoke to about seven hundred adults at a Valentine banquet. The audience roared with laughter throughout the evening. At the end of the evening I felt a little guilty that I didn't get "more heavy." After all, this was a church.

When I finished an elderly lady, her face still flushed from laughing, came up and clutched my hand. "I don't know how to thank you," she said, her eyes brimming with tears. "Three months ago I lost my husband after forty-five years of marriage. Tonight is the first time I have laughed since he died. I thought that life held no joy without him, but tonight you lifted that burden of depression from my soul." With a heartfelt thank-you she gave me one of the most rewarding hugs I have ever received.

Minutes later the pastor of the church drew me aside. (I am always a bit leery when a pastor draws me aside.) He told me how the church had been going through difficult conflict. "This . . . this . . . ," he struggled to find the right word, ". . . cleansing we experienced tonight is just what we needed." A letter that followed a few weeks later confirmed that the evening had served as a catalyst for some serious reconciliation and a new spirit of cooperation among the members of his congregation.

I'm not suggesting that humor is the answer to every problem; however, there are times when humor breaks down the barrier that keeps people from seeing solutions. Humor is just plain good for you.

2. HUMOR SOFTENS THE HEART.

In the foreword to my book *How to Speak to Youth . . . and Keep Them Awake at the Same Time,* Tony Campolo recalled a time when humor broke the stiff-necked spirit of a group of teenagers and opened their hearts and ears to listen. After an evening of laughter and inspiration Tony said this of the audience he felt had been unreachable the night before:

The atmosphere at the convention changed. The next morning the young people greeted me with rapt attention. They hung on my every word. . . . Ken Davis had done more than just entertain, he made the kids want to listen and respond. He set the stage for one of my most positive experiences in speaking to a group of young people![2]

I have lost count of the times I have stood before a hostile audience only to see them soften and become receptive because of the appropriate use of humor. It works whether the audience is six or sixty.

In a reversal of the situation mentioned above where a church asked me to come solely to make people laugh, I was once invited to a business luncheon for the sole purpose of presenting a message of faith. After I came and spoke before several hundred successful businessmen, one man wrote to say,

I came prepared to be offended by the religious nature of your talk. I wouldn't have been there at all but for a friend who coerced me into going. I was so disarmed by the delightful humor that I forgot to be offended. Before I had a chance to put up my armor I was deeply moved by the truth you presented. My friend and I talked all the way home and I prayed to trust Christ for the first time in my life. Thank you for presenting the truth in a way that could reach someone like me.

3. HUMOR PROVIDES INSTANT FEEDBACK.

It is not always easy to tell when you have lost the attention of an adult audience. When you lose teenagers they will roll their eyes, begin to play a miniature game of touch football, or text the content of their lives to a friend. But polite, savvy adults know how to shut you out, keep looking at you, and plan next month's vacation.

When people laugh or chuckle or just nod their heads in recognition of the funny truth, they are no longer benchwarmers. They have responded. That move from observer to participant imprints whatever you are communicating deep within the soul. Chances are much greater that they will remember and act upon what you present.

If you tell a humorous story that is tied to a truth you are trying to drive home, the audience response will give immediate feedback as to how well you connected. Silent stares or painful moans are an indication you have not done well. Laughter, smiles, and knowing nods indicate that the humor and the point connected to it have been heard and more importantly understood. Some speakers don't want to know when they are failing. I believe it is an opportunity to evaluate my speech on the fly and take advantage of the opportunity to adjust my delivery.

4. HUMOR RAISES THE DEAD.

It provides an audible, physical, and mental break that snaps an audience back to attention. In a sense, it allows the audience to take a breath and process what they've already heard. Many of the best speakers use humor at regular intervals in their presentations because they understand its power to bring the wandering mind back to attention even when the audience doesn't seem to respond.

Once, while making a presentation in the Northeast, I found myself speaking to an audience that didn't seem to be present. There was no visible evidence that they were listening to what I was saying. Some stared out the window. Others just looked in my direction without any expression. I tried my best humor to get them to respond, but except for an occasional chuckle, it seemed I was getting nowhere. I was particularly disturbed by an elderly gentleman who sat in the front row with arms and legs crossed. Judging from the furrow that he kept in his brow, it was lucky his eyes didn't cross. His body language indicated that he wasn't about to enjoy any part of this program. After a very long hour of intense work with little visible response, I finally closed the program.

The man with the furrow in his brow cornered me by the door. "That was the funniest program I ever heard," he said. "I thought I was going to die." It took all of my willpower not to respond, "I thought you had already died."

Then he topped off his comment by saying, "It was all I could do to keep from laughing." Even in this community where laughter seemed uncommon, the audience enjoyed the humor. They just tried very hard not to show it.

The point of this true illustration is that even when you are not aware of it, humor is bringing people to life. It recharges batteries and gives the audience the attentive capacity to handle your message.

WHAT MAKES SOMETHING FUNNY?

That's a serious question. If you know what makes something funny, you can use that knowledge to make anything funny. Some books go into explicit, hair-splitting detail about what makes people laugh. This chapter simply looks at the broad principles so that, without a degree in psychology, you can use those principles to bring humor to your presentations.

THE TRUTH

Some of the best humor is the humor born of simple truth. Remember our discussion of how the best illustrations come from real life. I believe the best humor comes from the observation of real life. Few people realize that simply pointing out truth can bring laughter. Consider these: A sign in a jewelry store says: "Ears pierced while you wait!" The average person never gives that a second thought. The person looking for humor realizes the ridiculous nature of that sign. (Of course you have to wait there to get your ears pierced. You don't have the option of leaving them and picking them up later.) Or the one at the summit of a fourteen-thousand-foot mountain that warns the driver "Hill." I suppose that sign is there to keep drivers from mistaking a fourteen-thousand-foot climb for a speed bump. What makes these signs funny is that they exist.

I often point out to parents that we take ourselves too seriously. When I remind parents of some of the silly things they say, they laugh as they recognize the truth. How many times has a parent shouted some admonition like, "Hey, if you cut your legs off in that lawn mower, don't you come running to me"?

I laughed out loud at my own ignorance one day when I cornered my teenage daughter and asked, "Do you think I'm stupid?" I suddenly realized that I didn't want a truthful answer. Judging from the laughter of audiences who hear this story, I am not the only one who has asked that question.

Humor that comes from simple truth is low-risk humor. Even if people don't laugh, the truth still remains. If that truth is tied securely to the rationale or objective of your message, its purpose is well served whether the audience caught the humor or not. When I ask students at the SCORRE Conference if they have ever heard Bill Cosby tell a joke, almost every hand in the class goes up. But the truth is, they have probably never heard Bill Cosby tell a joke because Cosby rarely tells jokes. He talks about real life. His portrayal of family situations and the remembrance of his childhood are simple recollections of truth exaggerated and made funny by his unique sense of humor.

The craziness of bureaucracy is suddenly center stage when the speaker mentions the warning tag on his mattress that threatens five years in prison and a ten-thousand-dollar fine if it is removed. Truth is funnier than fiction.

RIDICULOUS EXAGGERATION

This is the kind of humor most often associated with stand-up comedy. It is very visual and less cerebral than other types of humor. It is high-risk in nature because it will be obvious to the audience that you are trying to be funny. If it fails, it can be embarrassing and can become a barrier to communication. This is not the kind of humor for beginners or the faint of heart, and there are situations where this kind of humor may not be appropriate.

My dad used to say, "If you're going to make a scene, be seen." Exaggerated humor requires total commitment of mind and body and often must be accompanied by exaggerated facial expressions and unique voice inflections. A joint session of Congress or a convention of rocket scientists might not be enhanced by such humor but it might be perfect for a youth leader to grab the attention of his students. Regardless of the situation, this is the kind of humor that must be done well in order to succeed.

Examples of exaggerated humor are most often found with outright comedy. Bill Cosby screws up his face and threatens to run over his son because he brought the car home without filling it with gas. Steven Wright wonders out loud whether some skeletons might have a human hiding in their closet. Jerry Seinfeld refuses to be in a relationship with a woman with big hands. These are all hilarious routines that make full use of exaggeration. They are often limited to performance situations and require exceptional confidence and skill to be effective.

Your own personality and communication situation may eliminate most exaggerated humor from your repertoire. Don't let that discourage you. If you can't sing opera, there are many other kinds of music you can use to express yourself. Similarly, you can find humor that fits your style and situation even if you never use exaggerated comedy-style humor.

SURPRISE, SURPRISE

The kind of humor most often used in the telling of a "joke" is humor based on surprise. The punch line is a line that often takes the listener in a direction opposite of the direction the story was leading. It is the clever surprise of this punch line that tickles the funny bone. This kind of humor is also high-risk but does not require the same level of skill that exaggerated humor does. It is acceptable in a wider range of communication situations.

I broke a mirror the other day and heard I was supposed to get seven years of bad luck. My lawyer thinks he can get me off with three.

A lady who continually refused to fly because of fear was challenged by her son, "Your refusal to fly shows the weakness of your faith," he exhorted. "Jesus said that he would be with us always."

"No, he didn't," the woman retorted, "He said, 'Low, I am with you always.'"

There are many other subtle forms of humor, including special plays on words and unique definitions, but almost all of them fall into one of the categories above. It is also important to note that much humor makes use of a combination of the elements I've described. If you experience something you wish to share with your audience, you can use the principles already suggested to make it funny.

A little boy working on a report for school laid down his pencil and inquired of his mother, "Mom, where did I come from?" The mother had intended to talk with her son about this subject but was too busy at the moment so she responded, "The stork brought you." Finding his grandmother in the living room, he asked, "Grandmother, where did I come from?" Grandmother was not about to broach this subject, so she responded, "The stork brought you just like he brought me and your mother." The boy went back to his room, picked up his pencil, and began his report with these words: "There hasn't been a normal birth in our family for three generations."

Arrange the telling of your story so the surprise is saved until last and never hinted at.

When I heard this story, I burst out with laughter at the surprise of the ending. How much less effective this would have been if the speaker had simply said, "A boy once thought that his family was abnormal because they told him the stork brought him." It is the setup, timing, and surprise delivery of the punch line that make the story work.

Arrange the telling of your story so the surprise is saved until last and never hinted at. Purposely lead people in the wrong direction. If you give away the surprise, you telegraph the punch line and forfeit any laughter. They see it coming. Even when using simple truth for humor, try it out on your friends before you deliver it in public. Learn to tell your story in such a way that it maximizes the principles that will make it funny.

GET SERIOUS ABOUT HUMOR

Following are some considerations important to the communicator who wants to develop humor.

KNOW YOUR OWN STYLE AND ABILITY

Many are reluctant to try humor because they believe that to be humorous you must be a comedian. However, many excellent communicators who use humor are not naturally funny people. I have come to accept gratefully the fact that God has made me a funny person. Many times people laugh when I say things that I don't even consider funny. I enjoy making people laugh and find it quite easy, but you don't have to have a twisted mind like mine to use humor.

The range of humor extends all the way from wit that elicits a knowing nod to comedy that triggers uncontrollable laughter. Somewhere within those boundaries you will find humor that is consistent with your own style and ability.

Whatever you do, it is important that you don't try to be someone you are not. If you are not a naturally funny person, the humor you use will probably be closer to intellectual wit or poignant real-life anecdotes than outright comedy. Some of my favorite humorists are people who would never make it as a stand-up comedian.

Mark Twain had a dry, satirical wit that also conveyed intelligence and wisdom, yet I don't think there were a lot of belly laughs in response to his speeches.

One of my favorites, Will Rogers, elicited laughter yet remained dignified and intelligent in his delivery. "I don't belong to an organized political party," he said. "I'm a Republican!"

Tony Campolo uses a unique and dynamic delivery that is peppered with exaggeration, surprise, and truth. He uses the full range of humor to communicate a very serious message to a conservative audience. "I know what you are looking at," he says rubbing his bald head. Giving it one last rub he grins and says, "This is a solar collector for a sex machine." A younger man might not ever get away with it, but Tony knows his audience and brings the house down.

Even Billy Graham frequently used humor in his presentations, but you never heard him use weird voice inflections or saw him try exaggerated facial expressions, because for him that would be totally out of character. The same can be said for a sitting president. Many of them made great use of humor, but restricted their humor to the kind that maintained the dignity of the office. Be yourself.

DON'T SET YOURSELF UP FOR FAILURE

All humor can be divided into two basic categories: high-risk humor and low-risk humor. High-risk humor is the kind that demands a response of laughter. An obvious joke or exaggerated humor falls into this category.

If you stand in front of an audience and announce, "I heard a good one the other day, you're going to love it," you are attempting high-risk humor. If the audience doesn't laugh at the end of your story, there is going to be an embarrassing silence that comedians call death. It doesn't matter that you don't consider yourself a comedian; if you set your audience up for laughter and don't deliver, you will die just like a comedian. Surprising your audience with humor is so much better than dying in front of them.

Even without an introduction some jokes and stories are high-risk. Consider telling a story that begins like this: "One day a snail walked into a bar and crawled up on a stool." You are already in high-risk territory. The very concept of the story tips your audience that this is a joke and it's supposed to be funny. Now you've got to deliver. When humor fails, it hinders communication, takes a painful slice out of the speaker's self-esteem, and can stunt growth.

For that reason I suggest you use low-risk humor to start with. There are two kinds of low-risk humor. The first includes jokes and stories that are so good they never fail. Those are few and far between. Test them first and practice your timing before you deliver them in a critical situation. Even a sure-fire story can be ruined with a sloppy delivery.

The second kind of low-risk humor is the best. This type of humor is composed of true stories or other illustrations that carry their own weight even if no one laughs. Humor born of truth falls into this category. These kinds of stories are perfect for developing humorous skills because you have nothing to lose.

Our four-year-old daughter threw her hip against our bedroom door one morning and with indignation announced, "I've had a tooth under my pillow for three days." With her hands firmly planted on her hips, she groused, "If the fairy doesn't come tonight she is going to be missing some teeth of her own." Then she turned on her heel and left the room.

I have used this story to illustrate how quickly we lose patience, also to illustrate the impact of shattered expectations. Most of the time it gets laughter, but even when it doesn't nothing is lost. It is low-risk humor, and the story stands on its own as a good illustration. Low-risk humor also gives you the opportunity to try it more than once, practicing your timing and delivery, perhaps adding a bit of exaggeration until you get it right. Just be sure you don't deliver your story and then wait for laughter. Doing that immediately turns a low-risk situation into a high-risk situation. If you expect laughter and it doesn't come, just continue without pausing. We call that damage control.

BE AWARE OF THE DOUBLE EDGE OF HUMOR

Humor is like a double-edged sword. One edge can be used to build up and encourage, and the other edge can be used to destroy. You must be very careful to know which edge of the sword you are wielding. It is interesting to watch children use both sides of this sword with skill.

Teenagers will often adopt nicknames for each other derived from some perceived imperfection. A boy with large feet may be called "Shoes" by his buddies. This demonstrates that his friends recognize that he has big feet, but they like him anyway. A boy in my school walked through a plate-glass door and from that day forward was affectionately referred to as "Spook" because he had the ability to walk through walls. Yet teenagers use the same type of humor to ostracize and humiliate people they don't like. They know how to use both edges of the sword.

Some people contend that this kind of humor should never be used. I disagree. Among friends it is a way of showing intimacy and acceptance. However, it should never be used with strangers. What you meant to be a gesture of humorous acceptance can easily be taken as a cruel remark by someone you don't know. An audience that is not familiar with you may not take kindly to this kind of humor even if it is directed toward a friend. They have no way of knowing you are friends and simply conclude that you are insensitive and cruel.

In this regard ethnic humor is potentially lethal and should be avoided. Although you may have an ethnic friend in the audience with whom you are accustomed to making such exchanges, the chances are slim that the audience will accept such humor even if delivered with the best intentions.

I should caution you that you will not please everybody with your humor. If you use humor you are going to receive some criticism. The key is to know your audience and use humor that is appropriate. If you are unsure whether something is appropriate, it is probably good counsel not to use it. Remember, humor is a tool to enhance your communication. If you feel a story or joke might stand in the way of that communication, don't hesitate to eliminate it from your presentation.

For those of you who have chosen a ministerial profession, unfortunately you may find there are some who feel that humor has no part in any presentation of the gospel. If you are in a church where that view prevails, or if you find yourself in a situation where the audience would be offended if you used humor, deliver your speech with power and dignity and move on. In forty years of doing many presentations in churches, I have run into few people who are totally humorless and few churches that won't accept some humor even in worship. Appropriateness is the key.

Usually it's the style of delivery that determines whether it is appropriate or not. There are stories I use in concerts where I jump all over the stage, contort my face, and use strange accents. When I tell the same stories in other venues, I do so without all the accompanying body English and it's perfectly acceptable.

Two final pieces of advice:

1. WATCH OTHER PEOPLE.

Watch and learn from people who are experts at humor. Listen to how they get people to laugh by telling a story about something that most people have experienced. Stand-up comedians are not as valuable a resource as communicators who use humor well. Watch these people and see how they make their delivery. Be aware of the timing that can make or break humor and watch how the audience responds to different attempts at humor. When you see humor fail, ask yourself why and try to analyze how it might have been done differently.

2. PRACTICE, PRACTICE, PRACTICE.

Use friends, a spouse, or anyone who is friendly enough to listen. Begin to work low-risk humor into your presentations and don't be discouraged with occasional failure.

This entire chapter is devoted to humor because it is a powerful tool and well worth developing.

Recall Victor Borge's definition of humor: "The shortest distance between two people."

Exactly.

Characteristics of an Effective Communicator

The Messenger

Aristotle said that a good communicator must have the qualities logos, ethos, and pathos. Logos is associated with reasoning, logical order, and judgment. Of Aristotle's three appeals, logos—the sound foundation of reasoning to persuade the audience to belief, action, or intellectual consideration—was his favorite.

LOGOS

If you apply the principles of SCORRE described in the first part of this book, you will have satisfied the logos requirement. Those principles provide the organizational and logical foundation for a message that makes sense and has a sharp focus.

But logos is not enough. Every day thousands of charlatans, unethical scam artists, and political tyrants present powerfully focused, organized messages that destroy lives. If your concern is to communicate with excellence and enhance the lives of those who hear you, you must also have ethos and pathos.

ETHOS

Ethos, from which we get the word *ethics*, refers to the moral character and passionate belief at the source of a communicator's ability to persuade. A trusted and respected individual is more easily believed than one who does not demonstrate with his or her life what they are trying to communicate. Belief generates passion, and passion persuades.

There is an enthusiasm that accompanies the message of a speaker who deeply believes what she is saying. There is a genuine quality to the presentation of a salesperson who believes his product will enhance the quality of his perspective buyer's life.

This kind of enthusiasm is difficult to fake and almost impossible to hide. Not even the wonderful techniques in this book can substitute for a passionate belief in what you are presenting. There is such an obvious difference between the speaker who searches for messages because it is his job to deliver them and the speaker who can hardly wait to share what she believes.

Belief generates passion, and passion persuades.

It is a heady experience to be able to hold the attention of an audience. You have the power to use the audience to feed your own ego, or you can choose to enhance the quality of their lives. When you care, it shows.

PATHOS

Pathos refers to the communicator's ability to touch feelings, to move people emotionally. Pathos is not about toying with people's emotions for your own benefit. It has to do with using words, stories, and illustrations that demonstrate an empathetic awareness of the needs and feelings of your audience.

Choose words and illustrations that access the heart. When a person

LEARNING DOMAINS

is touched emotionally, that person is much more likely to consider your proposition and your reasoning.

Logos, ethos, and pathos must all be present in the life and performance of the effective communicator.

Closely related to Aristotle's appeals are the learning domains acknowledged by educators. These are represented in the above figure.

The cognitive domain is what we know. It is the sterile accumulation and dissemination of facts. The affective domain is what we feel. This domain can be accessed through truth or with lies. The motor domain is accessed by action.

It is very easy to concentrate on any one of these domains at the expense of the others.

An academic may find himself focusing on the cognitive domain, simply relaying great amounts of information in the mistaken belief that because he responds to raw data others will too. This kind of "cognitive dump" leaves the majority of the audience cold and unmoved.

A good storyteller will often concentrate on the affective domain. He knows he can use the emotion of a story to move people's feelings. But unless there is a logical foundation to support what is being communicated, people will quickly abandon whatever motivation was generated when the feelings have gone, or when someone else more dramatically accesses their feelings. (Think buyer's remorse.)

Finally, the activist will always have his audience doing something. Once again, action by itself will not carry the day. A passionate foundational reason for the action (logos) will sustain the action much longer.

As with Aristotle's appeals, the best learning takes place when the teacher/communicator accesses all three domains. The most effective communication takes place when there is a balance of information (cognitive, know) brought to life with illustration (affective, feel) and personalized with application (motor, action).

A careful study of Jesus' ministry reveals that he touched people emotionally. People responded strongly to his personal delivery of the truth. Some hated him, some loved him, but few ignored him. Some believed and others decided that he should be killed. He was presenting the most important cognitive truth in history. This truth had existed in the prophetic writings for years, but his pathos, his personal delivery, and his sacrificial application of that truth left no room for people to ignore him or sit idly by.

If you wish to communicate effectively, you will have to do more than just dump information on the audience or pepper the forest with logistical buckshot. The best messages can be heard, felt, and lived. Now you know the secrets of dynamic communication.

Live well, prepare with focus, deliver with clarity, communicate with power.

Appendix

EXAMPLES OF PROPOSITIONS

SUBJECT: SWIMMING
Persuasive: Every person should learn to swim.
Enabling: Every person can learn to swim.

SUBJECT: SALES
Persuasive: Every person should learn effective sales techniques.
Enabling: Every person can be more effective at selling.

SUBJECT: FEAR
Persuasive: Every person should face his/her fears.
Enabling: Every person can learn to face his/her fears.

SUBJECT: RELATIONSHIPS
Persuasive: Every person should pursue intimate relationships.
Enabling: Every person can develop intimate relationships.

SUBJECT: BELIEF IN GOD
Persuasive: Every person should believe in God.
Enabling: Every person can believe in God with confidence.

SUBJECT: MUSIC
Persuasive: Every person should listen to a variety of music.
Enabling: Every person can benefit from a variety of music.

EXAMPLES OF INTERROGATIVE RESPONSES

"Because of" and a key word (answers "why")

Arguments set forth
Tremendous **benefits**
Lasting **promises**
Doors that are **opened**
Issues at stake
Joys to be realized
Lessons to be learned
Needs to be addressed
Dangers to be avoided
People who are affected

Anxieties that can be relieved
Wounds that can be healed
Problems to be solved
Potential **rewards**
Historical **examples**
Costs of construction
Teachings of Jesus
Possible **consequences**
Relationships that are affected

These reasons will always be the key word when the interrogative response begins with the word "for." Example: Every person should invest in the stock market for three reasons.

"By" plus a verb and a key word (answers "how")

Following these **instructions**
Obeying two **commands**
Observing these **principles**
Avoiding several **traps**
Considering the **consequences**
Utilizing three **keys**
Claiming the **promises**
Making adequate **preparations**
Comparing three **women**
Asking two **questions**
Understanding the **limits**
Seeing the **possibilities**

Calming two **seas**
Tearing down two **walls**
Jumping two **hurdles**
Grasping three **straws**
Taming three **shrews**
Protecting four **treasures**
Guarding the **gates**
Planning important **strategies**
Playing these **games**
Cleaning the **closets**
Digging up three **bones**
Burying these **hatchets**

EXAMPLES OF KEY WORDS

abuses	directives	impressions	offenses
alternatives	divisions	issues	opinions
answers	doors	items	options
applications			orders
approaches	effects	joys	origins
areas	elements	judgments	
arguments	examples	justifications	parts
aspects	explanations		paths
assumptions	extremes	keys	penalties
assurances			perceptions
attitudes	facets	laws	perils
	factors	lessons	pictures
barriers	facts	levels	pieces
beginnings	faults	lights	places
beliefs	fears	limits	pleas
benefits	feelings	links	points
blemishes	flaws	loads	positions
blessings	forces	locations	possibilities
blots	forms		precautions
boundaries	fundamentals	marks	predictions
		measures	problems
causes	gains	memories	promises
challenges	gifts	mercies	proofs
changes	guides	methods	provisions
circumstances		models	
commands	habits	mountains	qualifications
comparisons	handicaps	mysteries	qualities
consequences	honors		questions
criteria	hopes	names	quests
criticisms	hungers	natures	
customs	hurts	needs	reactions
		norms	reasons
dangers	ideals	numbers	recommendations
declarations	ideas		records
definitions	idols	objectives	references
degrees	impacts	obligations	regulations
details	implications	obstacles	responses

restraints	solutions	thoughts	ventures
results	sources	ties	verifications
rewards	spheres	times	views
roads	statements	titles	violations
roles	states	tokens	virtues
	steps	tones	visions
sacrifices	stipulations	topics	vocations
satisfactions	stresses	traces	voices
sayings	strokes	trials	
scales	styles	triumphs	wants
scars	subjects	troubles	warnings
schemes	sufferings	truths	ways
schools	supports	types	weaknesses
seals	suppositions		weapons
seasons	symptoms	uncertainties	words
secrets	systems	undertakings	works
selections		units	worries
sentiments	tactics	urges	wrongs
sequences	talents	uses	
services	tasks		yokes
shields	teachings	vacancies	
situations	tendencies	values	zones
skills	tests	variations	
solicitations	theories	varieties	

POSSIBLE HEADINGS FOR TOPICAL FILE

Abuse
Advertising
Aging
Apologetics
Atheism

Bible
Boredom

Cheating
Christ
Christmas
Church
Communication
Competition
Confession
Conformity
Counseling
Creation
Crucifixion
Cults

Dating
Death & Dying
Discipleship
Doubt
Drugs

Easter
Ethics
Evangelism

Faith
Family
Fear

Forgiveness
Freedom
Friends

God
Growth
Guilt
Giving

Halloween
Heaven
Holy Spirit
Honesty
Hunger
Holiness

Jesus
Justice
Judgment

Legalism
Love

Marriage
Materialism
Media
Missions
Money
Morality
Movies

Obedience
Obesity

Parents

Peer Pressure
Phonies
Poverty
Prayer
Pride
Problems

Racism
Religion
Righteousness
Rock Music

Self Image
Sex
Social Concern
Scandal
Stealing
Suicide

Television
Temptation
Touching
Trust

Unity

Values

War
Will of God
Wisdom
Witnessing
Worldliness
Worry
Worship

SCORRE™ SPEECH WORKSHEET

SUBJECT: _____

CENTRALTHEME:_____

OBJECTIVE: _____

    PROPOSITION: Every _____ can/should

    _____ how/why

    RESPONSE: _____

Circle Key Word (plural noun)

RATIONALE:

    1) _____

    _____

    2) _____

    _____

    3)_____

    _____

RESOURCES:

_____

_____

_____

_____

EVALUATION:

Is my objective crystal clear? Is my key word a plural noun? Does it fit my rationale? Are my rationale parallel? Do my rationale lead to my objective?

Other Services and Materials Available from Ken

PERSONAL APPEARANCES

Ken Davis is one of the most sought-after communicators in North America. He is the award-winning author of ten books including *Fully Alive*. He is the host of *Lighten Up*, a syndicated radio show heard on over fifteen thousand outlets worldwide. His performances are a unique combination of side-splitting humor, inspiration, and life-changing truth. His energetic style and expert use of humor reaches people of all ages and backgrounds. An evening with Ken Davis will definitely make you smile. It may also change your life. For more information: www.kendavis.com.

CONFERENCES

Ken Davis is the founder of Dynamic Communicators International. He and Michael Hyatt, former chairman and CEO of Thomas Nelson Publishing, have recently teamed up to provide a series of seminars and workshops for speakers, writers, and communicators.

THE SCORRE CONFERENCE

Over the last three decades, Dynamic Communicators Workshops, now known as the SCORRE Conference, have helped thousands from all walks of life develop their speaking skills. Professional athletes, best-selling authors, corporate executives, and career ministry people are just among a few who have attended over the years. No matter what your present experience level, if you speak, these workshops are guaranteed to help you prepare and deliver presentations with clarity and confidence.

Workshop faculty from across the United States represents the top of the communication field. They also share the common attitudes of care and concern that will inspire you to develop your speaking skills. For more information: www.scorreconference.tv

THE PLATFORM CONFERENCE

If you want to make a scene, you have to be seen. The Platform Conference is based on Michael Hyatt's *New York Times* best-selling book *Platform: Get Noticed in a Noisy World*. This event teaches the invaluable skills that will get you seen and heard. If you have something to say or something to sell, this conference will help you build the platform to get the word out. For more information: www.platformconference.tv

THE LAUNCH CONFERENCE

If you have ever wondered how to monetize your communication skills or even make a career of what you love doing most, LAUNCH is a conference designed to teach you the business of speaking, writing, and entertaining. Ken Davis and Michael Hyatt have both built careers on their unique gifts and passions. At the LAUNCH Conference, they freely share the secrets that allowed them to do so. They have developed a trained and experienced team that will help you shape your message, get it in the marketplace, and perhaps launch your career. For more information: www.launchconference.tv

For further information or to register for any of these conferences, go to www.DynamicCommunicators.com. You can also get information by contacting:

Dynamic Communicators International
P.O. Box 681568
Franklin, TN 37068
(615) 599-8955

For the most up-to-date information on Ken Davis's CDs, books, DVDs, and other training resources, please visit www.kendavis.com.

Notes

CHAPTER 1
1. Haddon Robinson, *Biblical Preaching* (Grand Rapids, MI: Baker Academic, 1980), 33.

CHAPTER 2
1. Lowell Thomas, heard by Ken Davis in a speech delivered by Thomas.

CHAPTER 3
1. John Henry Jowett, *The Preacher, His Life and Work* (New York: George H. Doran Company, 1912), 133.

CHAPTER 7
1. Richard Lacayo, "Olympics: The Fall and Rise of Dan Jansen," *Time*, February 29, 1988, 87.

CHAPTER 8
1. *Bottom Line*, March 30, 1985, 6.

CHAPTER 12
1. Norman Cousins, *Anatomy of an Illness as Perceived by the Patient: Reflections on Healing and Regeneration* (New York: Norton, 1979), 43–44.
2. Ken Davis, *How to Speak to Youth . . . and Keep Them Awake at the Same Time* (Grand Rapids: Zondervan, 1996), 10.